MW00899312

Wake Up—God's Talking to You

Manny Dean Fernandez

WESTBOW°
PRESS
A DIVISION OF THOMAS NELSON
& ZONDERVAN

Copyright © 2014 Manny Dean Fernandez.

All rights reserved. No part of this book may be used or reproduced by any means, graphic, electronic, or mechanical, including photocopying, recording, taping or by any information storage retrieval system without the written permission of the publisher except in the case of brief quotations embodied in critical articles and reviews.

WestBow Press books may be ordered through booksellers or by contacting:

WestBow Press
A Division of Thomas Nelson & Zondervan
1663 Liberty Drive
Bloomington, IN 47403
www.westbowpress.com
1 (866) 928-1240

Because of the dynamic nature of the Internet, any web addresses or links contained in this book may have changed since publication and may no longer be valid. The views expressed in this work are solely those of the author and do not necessarily reflect the views of the publisher, and the publisher hereby disclaims any responsibility for them.

Any people depicted in stock imagery provided by Thinkstock are models, and such images are being used for illustrative purposes only. Certain stock imagery © Thinkstock.

ISBN: 978-1-4908-3018-6 (sc)
ISBN: 978-1-4908-3019-3 (hc)
ISBN: 978-1-4908-3017-9 (e)

Library of Congress Control Number: 2014904946

Printed in the United States of America.

WestBow Press rev. date: 05/07/2014

A moment of Dedication.

I'd like to make a dedication to a lifetime of writing [and waking at night] to my precious wife, Shar (Sharon) P Fernandez. How sad it was when she went to be with the Lord on December 13, 2013 from a sudden heart attack. I will miss her all the days of my life.

A dedication to my mother Helen (Apostalides) Fernandez who led me to our Lord, made me the kind gentleman I am today and who taught me how to listen to God. She only lived 40 years on this Earth and left us on July 26, 1976.

And finally, a dedication to my father, Manuel (Manny) Fernandez who spent a lifetime developing my intellect, as well as the order in my life and what God naturally gave me, a talent for numbers, business and giving Godly advice. I owe him my enduring love forever, he remains alive and well in Canton, Ohio.

Contents

Preface

Many years ago, I awoke suddenly in the middle of the night from a dream. I recalled every detail of that dream as I lay there in my bed in a state of shock and awe. I felt like the Spirit of God or even an angel of God had come upon me. Though the format of my dream was a little bizarre, I thought of it like a type of parable. It was sort of like a puzzle—a little weird yet very plain. My dream seemed a bit odd, yet at the same time, it made perfect sense.

You see, what had happened was this: God had revealed to me the dream's *exact meaning* the very moment I woke. I felt confident God had spoken to me, so I was excited and even felt a bit special. It was a sort of revelation in my own life. There wasn't a moment when I doubted this dream was from my Lord, not even for a second. *God had given me a dream!*

What I had just experienced was something very different in my life. It was so unusual yet so exciting, but you see—I had accomplished nothing; it was God who gave it to me. On that very special night, that dream impressed upon my mind the Spirit of God like I had never felt before.

The impact this dream left launched me into years of studying and documenting my dreams from that day forward. It was hard for me at first because I would wake up many mornings and not remember *a thing*. I was so frustrated. Then there were other days when He allowed me yet another wonderful experience of hearing from Him.

This, then, started me on a deep quest to study God's Word every day, every allowable moment I had.

Although in times past I had always read and studied the Bible, now I was devouring it! All of a sudden, I felt my life had a new purpose; I was indeed on a mission. My studies not only focused on my personal dreams, but I also looked into how God revealed Himself in both the Old and New Testaments using dreams and visions. I studied the lives and circumstances of all the people God spoken to ... in their dreams.

It sort of shocked me when I discovered that those who received dreams from God were not just His people but also those who did not even believe in Him. In fact, He gave meaningful dreams even to those who followed other gods. My studies revealed to me that God actually speaks to anyone and everyone in their dreams; so the question is, *do you know how to look for Him?*

As my dream diaries grew, I discovered that God *never* stopped delivering messages in people's dreams! At first I began to wonder, *did God stop talking to us, or did we just stop listening?* But now a new era has come upon us. I believe many of us feel we are now in what Christians call the latter days, and God's Word says, "In latter times old men will dream dreams and young men shall see visions."

This instruction book, as well as my diary of dreams, plus all the Scriptures associated with my studies, can now help launch *you* into an even deeper relationship and understanding of God. We will study the prophets of old and how their dreams came to them in a parable format just like mine do (and yours too). I will share with you how God gives *and also interprets* these dreams for me. You see, I've never interpreted my dreams; God reveals to me each and every one of them. I will also share with you why our dreams are at times so bizarre.

A very special note: You will never need another person to interpret your dreams; God and only *God* will *reveal,* or may I say untangle, your dreams for you. There will never be a need to call any eight hundred numbers. You won't need to go online. You will wake up and ask God to reveal the dream for you … and that is all you will ever need—only *God*! I'm going to teach you how to do that too!

We will also be studying the life of Jesus and how He, at times, even taught us things by using parables. Could it possibly be one reason Jesus spoke in parables was so we would have an understanding that maybe these same kinds of parables would come to us in our dreams?

Dreams are only one of the ways God speaks to us. This book, I believe, will assist you in developing a deeper relationship with the Father through the Holy Spirit, even as you sleep.

Since I began my nightly hunger for the Lord, it has taken me closer to God than I ever could have imagined. After giving half my life to this study, I am absolutely convinced God is speaking to *every single person* walking on this earth … in their dreams! I believe He even speaks to unbelievers because even though they don't believe, He is still their God and is still communicating to them in their dreams.

The Bible tells us plainly that in the latter days, men will dream dreams. And by the way—nothing the Lord God has ever spoken has not come true! This book just **may** be the instrument to teach you how to worship and understand Him in an even deeper and greater relationship—more than you could ever have imagined. This book will be a tool and instruction book to learn how to understand your dreams, as well as how God will interpret them for you. More importantly, it will teach you how to wake up and remember them! *We all dream, but it is the remembering that's the key.*

You will read about my successes as well as my failures: the good times, the hard times, and even the dry spells I suffered through. At times I found myself so nervous because during those dry spells, I thought, *Why has He stopped communicating with me?* I got through it, and I'll get you through it too.

I will share how God brought me through those rough times and how He meant the dry period (as I call it) to be a part of my training to share with you. You see, this book is all about God; it's not about me or you. The dreams come when He wants them to come, not when I want them to come. So my prayers, my fasting, and my hours upon hours of praying will be shared with you so you too will learn from my years of study, practice, and application.

In the later chapters, I will share how God taught me to pray and ask Him for specific answers to my prayers in my dreams. Each night I would have a specific prayer, and He answered those prayers as I slept. What a thrill and even a chill you will get from this study! I believe there will be times during these studies when *you will even cry!* Why? Because we Christians love the Lord so much, we simply hunger and thirst to know Him better and better. I believe there will be a time when you will simply pause and shed a tear, but be patient; it will all come together in time.

You will be able to take what took me years and condense my work into an almost instant association, as well as a nightly relationship with God. After completing this course, your nights will be filled no longer with simply sleep but a twenty-four-hour relationship *and* the greatest fellowship with Jesus Christ, our Savior and Lord. You will enjoy the peace and quiet of the night as well as a continued fellowship with Him during the day. I know this will be such a joy to you. It'll even bring that tear!

I will explain this further in the chapters to come, but before we get started, you must know this: *at no time will dreams take the place of reading God's Word or prayer!* Nothing has changed here, friends. I am just going to teach you and share with you how to enjoy Him even when you're sleeping. This has been one of God's ways from the beginning of time, so this is no new revelation but an old one.

The Bible has been feeding us for generations. It holds within it the codes and secrets to life. It seems that people are constantly looking for more answers to what will happen to the future of mankind. The Bible spells out for us that in latter times, certain things will occur. There will be famines, earthquakes, wars, and rumors of wars. Things like hunger, starvation, and death will fill the earth. There will be terrible violence in our society and even violence and hatred within our own families. Men will lead people away from God's true Word and the body of Christ (the church) will be broken into many pieces. Cults will form and take away innocent victims to follow their anti-Christian ways. This, of course, will only bring destruction to those who follow.

This book will attempt to help you get even closer to God. My goal is to help guide you into a deeper understanding of the things God set into motion thousands of years ago—a special communication channel to be with Him at night. Your spirit will converse with the Holy Spirit. God tells us He never changes, so why did we stop looking for Him in our dreams? He has been calling to us night after night (in repeated nightly dreams), but we have been blind to know that this was His voice. Once you have understood and interpreted a particular repeated dream, that dream will go away and be put to rest *just like that!* He has delivered His message, and you have received it. It is now time to move on to the next one, and He does!

God bless you all. I will pray each and every day that the years God has blessed me with, and that I have put into these pages, will be blessed in your life now, too. Read these pages carefully. Pray always, and remember, do not allow this *ever* to take the place of reading God's Word! It is still, and always will be, the number-one way to know God's will in your life. Now wake up and read; God is talking to you!

God bless you all.

—Manny Fernandez

CHAPTER 1

In the Beginning

In the last days, God says, I will pour out my Spirit on all people. Your sons and daughters will prophesy, your young men will see vision, your old men will dream dreams.

—Acts 2:17

I need to paint a picture for you of who I am before we begin so you will understand my personality as well as my character and even the kind of work I do.

Everyone who knows me will *unanimously* agree that I move at a pretty fast pace. Everything I involve myself with I do with a lot of energy and determination. It is not nervous energy but straight-up determination and zeal. Whether it's work or play, I establish goals, and when I set my mind to a project, I see it through.

I live each and every day with the peace only God can give, but boy, if there's a project out there that needs to be done, hand me the ball—I'm your man. As the saying goes, "Here I am, Lord, send me."

If I'm talking to someone on the phone, I'm also washing dishes at the same time. If there are no dishes to do, I will dust, pick up things, and straighten out the house. Sometimes I'll even type on the computer while talking on the telephone. My wife, Shar, calls me a fluffer, always fidgeting and never sitting still while on the tele.

At nearly fifty-five years old, I have as much energy as my grandson, Nicholas. Nick is a teen, and he calls me Papo. It's Greek for "grandfather." My mother was Greek, and my father is half-Spanish and half-Sicilian. I've got one great big boilermaker of blood running through my veins.

I have also been blessed with the world's greatest wife (she made me put that in here) who has dealt with my fidgety energy for nearly thirty years. With all my energy, shortcomings, past addictions, and problems, she deserves a reward! Shar and I have been on top, and we have also seen rock bottom. We have been through more trials and tribulations than I would ever want anybody to go through. God has made sure I have tasted and tested everything!

One of the ways Shar and I make a living is as entrepreneurs; we buy and sell businesses. Sometimes we open these businesses from their conception and then sell them to individuals who are looking to make a living from something we have nurtured into success. This is similar to a person who would buy and sell a fixer-upper home. They call this *flipping*. We also purchase rundown businesses; we clean them up, build them up, fix them up, and then sell them. That would be called a turnkey—where you buy a business that's ready to go, turn the key (in the lock), and you're ready to go. In the past twenty-some years, we have owned and sold about thirty profitable (and fun) businesses.

In fact, sometimes we operate more than one or even two at a time. When I get up in the morning to start my workday, I head to business number one, open it, run to the next one, and stay there for a while, then run to the next one or back to the first one and so on. My point here, and this is important, is I live life in the fast lane. I need you to get a picture of my busy life before we get going.

Now, are you ready for this? Believe it or not, business flipping is more of a hobby than my job. I make a living as an accountant. I have a private practice that cares for nearly one thousand families and businesses. You see, I found out many years ago that I have a God-given talent to make a business succeed. I felt early enough in life that instead of being greedy with this gift, I would share it with others by being their consultant, accountant, and friend. So my clients' businesses' success is as important to me as if I owned their business myself. I take great pride in my work, and because God gifted me with so much energy, taking care of just my own two or three businesses wasn't enough. I need to have more on my plate than even my own businesses … Now that's a lot of energy! Agreed?

But my businesses are not where I start each and every day. Before the crack of dawn, I'm on my knees. I can't see getting through a day without first acknowledging my Father who has given this day to me. I follow the formula of ACTS when I pray (adoration, confession, thanksgiving, and supplication), and that works for me. There's no right or wrong way to pray; God just wants to hear from us. I believe God is in heaven waiting each day for fellowship with me. I can choose to ignore Him, or I can make Him part of my life by talking with Him, consulting with Him, and simply making Him, my God, my consultant—a heavenly Father who is part of my everyday life.

After prayer, I take my morning shower and read God's Word before starting my fuel-injected engine—me. In fact, let me change something here. I don't read the Bible; I study it. The Bible is my lifeblood, and I can't imagine anyone who could go through life without that dose (fuel) of God's Word each and every day. Studying God's Word is more important to me than food or water. Shar and I also take time to read together later in the afternoons, after dinner. If I'm ever too busy and neglect reading for a day, I feel I have lost something. The only day I do not follow this regiment is on Sunday. Sunday is different.

I spend two hours on Sunday watching Charles Stanley. Doctor Stanley's messages on the television show *In Touch*, as well as that ministry, are such a blessing that I must watch his televised service *twice* to make sure it all sinks in. Dr. Stanley serves up so much meat at his table that I want to grasp and store everything he has to say. If you're eager to learn, just turn on your television set and almost every hour on Sunday morning you will find Dr. Stanley on one channel or another. I live in Riverside County of Southern California, and Dr. Stanley is on (at least) four times on Sunday and at least once on Saturday night.

After that blessing we, of course, go to church. I know Dr. Stanley, as well as any other television or radio minister, would want that of us too. Some might think watching church on television is enough, but that doesn't give you the fellowship that is so necessary for spiritual growth. I cannot count how many times I've heard people say, "I don't need church; church is in my heart, and there is nothing in church but a bunch of hypocrites." Whew, it's exhausting hearing that nonsense line from people who are simply too lazy or uncommitted to get up and find themselves a right place to worship for their family. Now I have a huge opportunity to respond to that excuse in a public forum.

Hog Wash

Going into a building to worship God, with others, is what life is all about. The worship part, my friend, is *you* singing songs and praising the Lord. The message brought to you by your pastor is not the worship; it is simply a short message after the worship to help you grow. The sermon is kind of like a Bible study. As far as standing on your couch at home and reaching up to heaven and singing songs in your underwear, forget it. The fellowship of being together with other Christians makes it a worship service to our Lord. To sit at home on your couch without attending church is just not the same. A one-man football team? Never heard of it!

Each one of us is but a tiny member of a huge body (1 Cor. 12:12–31). The body (the church) worships God in unity as a body. And as far as hypocrites at church are concerned, what in the world makes people think we Christians aren't human? Hey, man, I make more mistakes than you! But I sure don't call you a sinner or a hypocrite when you goof up. The only difference between a Christian and non-Christian is that we Christians understand this—and Jesus forgives us for our sins when we communicate with Him and ask Him to. We surely are not supermen! We are sinners who continue to goof up but are forgiven by our Father who is in heaven.

I've heard enough of that hypocrite talk already! My name is Manny, not Jesus. He died for my sins so I might have fellowship with God, the Father, and live my life through Jesus. Do you understand that? So I go to church to be with all the other people who say, "I, myself, will never be perfect, so let's do this together."

My church is where I find my extended family. These people love me and have taken me in and accepted me as a brother in Christ. These people look beyond my faults and see me as just another member of this family. None of us are perfect, but we are all forgiven. By the way, I actually have a few churches I like to attend, Gracepoint Nazarene in Wildomar, California, Bear Creek Calvary Chapel in Wildomar and Lakehills Baptist Church in Lake Elsinore, California. It is THERE where you find my family!"

Going to church is like putting gas in your car. We all need fuel, and if you think you can go through life without learning and growing in God's Word (fuel), you're wrong. And if you think you can stay home and read your Bible by yourself and not have a teacher, sorry, but you're wrong again. Oh sure, you can do it, but you won't be getting any feedback from others, hearing others' thoughts on what they get out of Scripture. You'll just be getting your own point of view and never knowing if you're right or wrong on your perspective of that Scripture you are reading. Going to church is one of the most important tools for being a well-fed Christian. (Okay, I'm done.)

Well today I'm not here to write stories about my life, per se, nor to vent my frustrations at the world ... or this country. What we are here to talk about are your dreams and how I am convinced (and will soon *prove* to you) that God is speaking to each and every one of us while we sleep.

I am not going to just tell stories here. That is not my agenda. But we will study some of God's Word and search through the Bible for both men and women who have had the experience of God speaking to them through their dreams. A little later, we will review some of my own dreams and why this study and the gathering of this book took as many years as it did. This book, and my work, were years in the making. The lifelong process necessary to step out in faith didn't come easy. I had to make sure of all the facts. This book took a lot of time and a lot prayer and *most of all*, a lot of studying of the precious Word of God.

I believe, as do most Christians today, that the end times are upon us. The Devil has raised the stakes, and now the Holy Spirit is ante-ing in as well.

Let us first take a look into the enemy camp.

The anger and rage in our society have never been as bad as it is at this time in history. Our judicial system is so wacky that the innocent get locked up and the guilty either go free or get out in no time flat. Some people are going to prison for twenty-five to life for stealing a pack of lifesavers and others who drive drunk and kill a pedestrian get out in four to seven. My friend Joe Musser got seven years for taking a woman's purse of her cart at shopping store. Was it wrong? You bet! Should he have gotten punished and locked up? You bet! But seven years? Wow, what a wacky system.

Our medical system is also so out of control that almost any major illness is going to break your bank. Shar and I pay hundreds of dollars each and every month just to fill our prescriptions. A visit to the emergency room, even for a minor issue, is going to cost you *thousands*. A friend of mine named Tony had cancer in his leg. When they discovered it, they wanted to operate immediately. It took his HMO six days to get an approval. In the meantime, Tony suffered in pain while we all prayed and waited for the insurance company to say okay. He nearly died.

A friend of mine was building a beautiful church in our community called Lambs Fellowship. The church burned to the ground in its last stages of construction. It took over one year, and the insurance companies were still fighting and placing blame. Nothing was being done about the restart of construction again ... *One year!* Today the church is open and doing *great*.

We seem to tolerate, year after stupid year, the promises our politicians make yet rarely fulfill. As dumb as we are, as a society, we continue to allow these men and women to repeat themselves—over and over and over. How dumb are we, you guys? How can we continue to listen and even *cheer* when we hear these politicians tell us what they're going to do, yet they don't *ever* live up to their campaign speeches? I watch on television the speeches and shake my head at an immature nation that believes this guy is really gonna bring change or reform. Promise after promise, year after year, campaign after campaign ... yet we still cheer and believe.

Today's television is also out of control. We now have shows with vampires, witches, werewolves, and other entities that are supposed to be our friends and entertain us. Oh yeah, they entertain all right—with sex. Each of these shows is nothing more than today's heroes who are now our sex symbols.

The movies that are made today show so much violence and bad ideals for children that it brings tears to my eyes. The odds today of a teen going through puberty without having sex are incredible.

Most video games today consist of killing. Blowing up asteroids is a thing of the past; now we must kill people on these video screens. Go to an arcade or a place that sells video cartridges, and all you can really buy is death, violence, and sex. That's what sells today.

Okay, enough of that; now let's explore the Holy Spirit's (God's) camp.

Never before has the Word of God reached the world as it does today. Good, strong, independent churches are opening under the simple name "Christian Church" rather than the old days where the churches were Baptist, Lutheran, etc. It seems like the body of Christ is coming together (once again) to do battle and prepare for the Groom to return (Jesus). Luke shares two Scriptures with us, in Acts telling us that Christianity was once called "the way," and I believe that name might soon be coming back. What is the way? This should be the question men ask today. We should not have any particular sect of Christianity but a *united way*.

It appears in church history that centuries passed with rare instances of the Holy Spirit's gift of speaking in tongues. Today the Holy Spirit is moving so strongly that the days of Pentecost are once again upon us. (Come quickly, Lord Jesus.)

God's Word is going out like never before, and churches are growing and being built rapidly. Today the buildings are being erected not with steeples and church bells but just large buildings with huge square footage to seat thousands and thousands of men, women, and children who wish to congregate and worship our Savior, Jesus.

Although I have authored this book, it took so many years that some would think I went a little overboard waiting to publish. I could have stopped writing a long time ago, but I had to be absolutely sure of what I am going to share with you. I constantly looked for God to tell me to move on. I was constantly aware that the counterfeiter would be upon me and attempt to influence my every word (Eph. 6:12) The Holy Spirit was my guide and I truly know it was He who guided me to write these words, using me as His vessel to bring this message.

I am going to share some dreams I've had and explain how I am convinced God is speaking to you in your dreams too. He says in the last days He will pour out His Spirit, and part of that pouring is in dreams and visions. I will spend most of the time in this book teaching you how to look for *and remember* those dreams.

My first dream, or might I say the first time I truly felt God was speaking to me in my dreams, occurred many years ago. This dream hit me so hard that it threw me into years of study. I had another dream that shook me not long after the first, then another and yet another. It wasn't long after those initial dreams when I decided to start writing them down, and it was then that I began my first of *many* diaries to come. I now have thousands of dreams logged into my diaries.

This study not only had good and memorable nights but bad nights, bad dreams, and even dry spells. (We will study nightmares later.) I soon discovered that I had to be *right*, *pure*, and *in prayer* to receive some of my better dreams. Let us now look at these three important factors before we begin.

Being right in the context above means right in prayer, heart, and mind and not being clouded by other things.

> *Come near to God and he will come near to you ...*
>
> (James 4:8)

That doesn't (necessarily) mean I had to pray to receive a dream. We all dream. But my dreams and the *quality of those dreams* got better when I started to recognize them as God speaking to me. The closer I got to God, the closer He got to me; then closer and even closer. It seemed I kept growing in the Lord, taking steps closer to Him. I felt His hand reaching out to me as I kept discovering Him at night in my dreams, so I sort of held my hand out to grab His. Later the dreams got even better when I started praying to God and conversing with Him *about those dreams.* I brought Him into my mind's conversation, acknowledged the dreams, and discussed them with Him. Part of my morning prayers would be to talk to God about the dreams aloud. He then acknowledged me back (not verbally) and gave me further dreams to talk to Him about. I found and believe that God enjoyed hearing from me and **especially the fact that I acknowledged receiving the message.** I truly, truly believe He is loving this as much as I am. It's like He's saying "Eureka, someone has finally got it! *Now,* go tell everyone else. There's plenty of this to go around. Go teach them how!"

Don't laugh at what I'm about to say, but try and think of this as sort of an e-mail worship or relationship with God, only in dreams. You answer your mail or e-mail, and you're now in the relationship. If you don't write me back or acknowledge me, you're not going to get many more messages. Acknowledge the first message (dream) and He will move on to tell you more and more and *yes, more!* I think it is the same with e-mails. If you answer my e-mail, I'm going to write you another and so forth!

When I stayed in prayer, my prayers were answered. When I stayed close to God, He got even closer to me. On the nights when I just went to sleep, I may have dreamed, but when I truly prepared for that night with prayers and petitions to my Father, asking Him, "Come and speak to me, Father," those particular nights were much, much closer to Him. We came together *and met in those dreams.*

One of the hardest stages of my testing was when I purposely, let's say, ignored God (or a closer relationship with Him) to go to sleep for periods of time *just to* see if He would come to me. Now I don't literally mean I forgot God; I just purposely went to sleep, ignoring the intimacy to test my theory in the early stages. (I did this again several times throughout the years to test my theory.) What happened was I found myself going through withdrawals, missing Him every night.

> *So I say to you: Ask and it will be given to you; seek and you will find; knock and the door will be opened to you. For everyone who asks, receives; he who seeks, finds; and to him who knocks, the door will be opened.*

(Luke 11:9)

Pure is the second part of this study. This too got better as I tested, experimented, and discovered these dreams. I had to stay as pure as I possibly could to receive the best dreams from God. To help you understand this, allow me to further explain. I am a heavy man. I am overweight around the belly. The rest of my body is in relative proportion to my frame, but I do have myself a belly! I would often munch, snack, and nibble most evenings as I would read or watch television. Well, I found later on that on an emptier stomach, my dreams would be of better quality, or maybe I should say I was more ready for the dreams.

I believe we sleep differently when we are full, on medication, or even intoxicated. When I use the word *pure*, I don't mean virginal or spiritually perfect; I mean more emptied of bodily functions and pure in mind. But now that I have mentioned virginal, I should mention that sex had nothing to do with receiving or not receiving dreams. I had to test that too, you know. But sex between married couples is a natural act of God. He never hindered my prayers or my dreams because of having or not having sex. I think this is important to mention, folks, because I would not want a couple's relationships to be hindered (or cause problems) because one of you is looking for this deep, intimate relationship with God at night and the other might not. I wouldn't want you to cut off relations with your spouse to "be pure," so I felt it necessary to explain that for *years* I studied this part of dreaming, after having sex as well as not having sex.

Let's move on. After a lot of reading and being familiar with God and fasting, I came to realize that when I fast, I am more in tune with God than when I don't. I believe all people who have fasted should know this, so this is no big secret or discovery. When our bodies are emptied of all those toxins, we just seem to be more in tune spiritually. I am not saying here that if you have a bowl of ice cream before bed, God will not allow you dream communication with Him. All I am saying is that the cleaner or emptier *my* body was at night, the better I seemed to dream.

In conclusion, I'm not telling you to fast before sleep. This doesn't make sense because we sleep every day, we dream all the time, and we have to eat. All I'm concluding here is that the distance between your last meal and bedtime makes a little bit of difference in your (my) dreams. I am just explaining a study I conducted over a period of many years; I am in no way suggesting that you must fast from food to hear from God!

Last, I mentioned that I had to be in *prayer*, and this should go without saying. If you believe in God, then praying has always made us closer to the Creator. Not too much should have to be said about prayer. It is our communication link to the Father. Living my life without prayer is like living my life without air. Even when I didn't talk to God about my dreams, I still prayed in the morning and throughout the day on a regular basis. If you're a Christian, can you imagine not praying? Wow, what a *rush* to even think that. That's like leaving home without a shower or clothes ... or at least it better be. So enough said about that; let's move on again.

When I first began my study, I didn't remember my dreams every night. In fact, I still don't. It took a while for me to get familiar with dreaming and how God wanted to communicate with me. It was the first few dreams (in the beginning) that made me sure He was there and speaking to me. Let's just say I had to sort of practice to begin to remember most of my dreams. Some people are already really good at remembering dreams, but for me, it took time, practice, and patience. It also took many forms of experimenting. In the beginning, once I had a few special dreams, I was really excited and ready for more.

In the early stages, I would get very frustrated when I'd wake up and know I had had a dream but couldn't remember much of it. I would remember bits and pieces but not all of it. I got really frustrated. It was like reading half of a letter. I really got upset at myself, but this was part of God's teaching all along. Then on other mornings, I would wake joyfully, with pen in hand, ready to write down all or most of my dream. You can believe me when I say this took practice, as well as patience and prayer. I hope to get *you* through this easier than what I had to go through because I tried it all. I'm going to give you the shortcuts and help you to do this in a lot less time than it took me. Of course I learned from my mistakes, and now I can pass those along.

In a few minutes, we're going to look at my first dream. This first dream was short and sweet, but as soon as I woke up, I immediately felt something in me say, *"This dream was from God."* Of course I have been dreaming for years, since I was a baby, I guess. But I think what happened was that I woke up and felt that God had just given me a message or was telling me, "It is time to start learning, teaching, writing, and shouting from the mountaintops." Now here is that first dream. Don't blink or you'll miss it.

I was driving a car and passing everybody on the road. I was zigging and zagging and just driving like a maniac. As I passed many cars and trucks, not only was I on the road, but I drove off the road and onto the grass to pass everyone I possibly could. Then I came up on this bus at a very high speed. I began to pass the bus, and all of a sudden the bus driver stuck his head out of the driver's window and yelled out, "Drive as fast as you want, but don't ever pass me! Always stay behind me." Then he yelled out real loud, *"Always!"*

When I woke up, this was my first thought: *The car, and me in it, was the pace of my life.* (This is one reason why I had to share my personality with you.) *The bus, I believed (and felt), was God's Word, and the bus driver was God.*

How did I know this? I just did! It was an immediate feeling I had deep inside of me. I was immediately and simply positive of my analogy. There was no doubt in my mind. I felt so confident in the interpretation of this dream that I sat up in my bed in a state of awe! I woke up with my jaw wide open and thought to myself, *I just heard from God.* In fact, I was even a little shaken by the experience.

God was telling me that He always wanted to be ahead of me and that I am never to try and pass Him. He wanted to always lead me and be ahead of me at all times and in everything pertaining to my life. He simply wanted to be first! The bus (the Word of God or the Bible) was also to be foremost in my life. The dream expressed that God Himself and His Word should always be in front of me, and I was never try to pass Him, so to speak. No matter how fast-paced my life was, I had to put God and His Word first!

I am so confident that God speaks to *all of us* while we sleep that we will need to study many aspects of this subject carefully. This is not going to be a book of my opinions either. If you remember in the preface, I explained how this took years to compile. Hence I will share my studies with you, and then you can draw your own conclusions.

Well that was it—the first dream. In the chapters to come, this book will contain several of my dreams, how I learned to remember them, and most importantly, how you can too. I mentioned earlier that this was not an overnight accomplishment. Being in tune with your dreams takes a mental, conscious awareness, and that takes practice. In my case, it took years to sort of master it. I had dreams every night (I guess), and so do you, but to learn just about anything in life, we must be taught. I believe all people have the potential to have this communication with God once they learn how, so let's get started!

In today's evangelical church, we talk about the subject of gifts of the Spirit (1 Cor. 12:1–11). Some people believe these gifts may have left the people of this world shortly after the original pioneers (the apostles) of the way (Acts 9:2, 19:9; later they were called Christians, Acts 11:26b) passed on.

The gifts of the Spirit would include miracles, speaking in tongues (this is an indescribable language or communication between the person praying and God), laying on of hands to cure or help cure a sick person, prophecy, and more.

Before we get too deep into this, here is how to look things up in the Bible, in case you are unfamiliar. First get a Bible, because you're going to need one if you want to follow along with this study. Then you go to the area of the Bible (or book in the Bible) that I will designate. In this case it would have been 1 Corinthians. Then the next number would be the chapter within that book, which, again, in this case is chapter 12. The last number after the chapters after a colon would be the verse or verses. In this case the verses were 1 through 11. So it reads (1 Cor. 12:1–11).

I have three more things we need to discuss before we really get going, so let's take a look at them one at a time. The first thing is for you to understand what I mean by gifts of the Spirit.

Some people believe the gifts of the spirit are no longer in the world. These people believe that these gifts, like speaking in tongues, laying hands on people to heal them, and other gifts, left the church (or the world) shortly after the original apostles died. Most *know* by proof in their own lives and/or by personal witnessing that these gifts of the Spirit are alive and well here on planet earth. We see them every day! What makes some believe they are gone and others say they are still here? Good question. Basically it is in the use or nonuse or calling of the Spirit. If you don't use something or do not learn how to use that something, then you will never understand it. Take the keen senses of a blind person. The blind person's other senses are acutely more in tune with her body because she uses those senses more than a person who is not blind. The Holy Spirit and His gifts are sort of like that. Use them, look for them, and you'll find them.

As a child, when I attended the Greek Orthodox Church, worship was very different from the church I now attend. Although the church I attend today is basically a non-charismatic church, the Spirit seems to be more active (to me anyway) now than when I attended the Holy Trinity Greek Orthodox Church. And if I would visit, let's say, a Pentecostal Church, the Spirit there might move more vigorously than even my own church. So what's the difference? The way in which each church chooses to worship. Therefore that is *one reason* why there are so many different types of churches and denominations today. Truly, it is a matter of personal preference.

I do not really want to say this, but I'm going to. I believe if you put a Pentecostal service in a Catholic church, they too would be praising God in the aisles rather than in their seats. It is not the type of church as much as the type and style of worship you prefer.

The second preface to look at prior to beginning our actual study is to recognize the number of times God spoke to people in their dreams. In both the Old and New Testaments, God came to so many people in a dream that if you didn't get a message from God in a dream, you must have stayed up all that night and not slept (just a joke).

> *At Gibeon the Lord appeared to Solomon during the night in a dream, and God said …*

(1 Kings 3:5)

God not only came to His people in dreams, but He spoke in dreams to those who did *not* follow Him or worship Him. They too were visited by Him as He attempted to give them a message in their dreams, though their dreams were not always pleasant. Today we might call them nightmares. In those days, the people sort of automatically knew God was talking to them in their dreams! They didn't really look upon these dreams as mere nightmares. These men knew right away that there was a message from God. So what happened to us? Why did we go off and forget this?

Joseph, for example, was to interpret Pharaoh's dream in Genesis 51:15:

> *Pharaoh said to Joseph, "I had a dream, and no one can interpret it. But I have heard it said of you that when you hear a dream you can interpret it."*

Pharaoh could have just wakened on those mornings and said, "Man, what a wild nightmare I just had," but he didn't! He not only felt that his dreams had meanings, but he also sought counsel *all over the land*, seeking for someone to interpret those dreams. What makes you think Pharaoh and all the rest of those guys were so different than you and me?

Pay attention when Pharaoh also mentioned, "I have heard it said," when he was talking to Joseph. What does that sound like? Was this, then, Joseph's first experience? Or could it be that while Joseph was in prison (for all that time), he may have had the time to get in tune with himself and see that God spoke in his dreams as well as the dreams of the others in prison with him? It sounds to me like Joseph had himself one great reputation. Did his fellow inmates often ask him to interpret their dreams? Did the prison guards, too, catch wind of this and spread the rumor and reputation that Joseph could interpret dreams? And more importantly, was Joseph the only one in the world who could do this? Evidently not! Pharaoh sought out other dream interpreters who could not produce the correct answers. I will explain a little later why they couldn't interpret them.

Now here's another; Pontius Pilate's wife "suffered" greatly in a dream in Matthew 27:19. Her dream was sort of a haunting or nightmarish dream of Jesus.

> **While Pilate was sitting on the judge's seat, his wife sent him this message: Don't have anything to do with that innocent man, for I have suffered a great deal today in a dream because of him.**

> (Matt. 27:19)

My point here is this: Some of these people were not only Gentiles (not Jewish), but they also were not followers of God. *But still they had dreams and messages from God.* Also notice that these dreams occurred both in the New and the Old Testaments. Some of you who study the Bible will continue to insist that these things ended. Again, was the Spirit of God taken away? *No way.* He came in dreams in the Old Testament, and He came in the New Testament. He comes to you today, and His Word now states that He is promised to come to many in the last days.

God *still* speaks to us in our dreams, and I am going to *teach you that so you will learn how to look for God in your dreams.* Now, if you're going to study this subject *more* than just reading my book, before we move any further, take a *Bible concordance* and look these words up and study them: dream, dreams, and dreamed. Then look up vision and visions. I'll see you tomorrow! This will take quite a bit of time, but you will have much better knowledge and understanding before we move on.

A Bible concordance is a reference book to help you look up words and see where those words are within the Bible. There are so many places to look up in the category of dreams. It will take a very long time to read them all, and I will not write them all down here as well. For the sake of time, space, and repetition, first study through your concordance and then come back to your bookmark on this page.

Now, if you just did that, isn't it is safe to say that God spoke to many people in a *whole lot of dreams?*

The third and maybe the most important factor I want to cover before our actual study comes from Jesus life on earth. When Jesus walked on this earth, He told many of His stories in the form of parables, and I am sure most of our dreams come to us in parables. Parables tell a story not in a direct way, but if you have any awareness of God, then you know that the Holy Spirit opens your mind to understand the parable, and then the story will unfold. A parable is sort of an earthly story with a heavenly meaning. If you have no knowledge of God at all, then you might be confused by parables. Look up parables in Matthew 13:34 and Mark 4:10–12, just to try out a few. There are a lot more to find in the New Testament gospels (books) of Matthew, Mark, Luke, and John.

> *He told them, "The secret of the kingdom of God has been given to you. But to those on the outside everything is said in parables so that, they may be ever seeing but never perceiving, and ever hearing but never understanding; otherwise they might turn and be forgiven!"*
>
> (Isa. 6:9–10)

19

Jesus came to this earth and spoke in parables, and God spoke to so many people in bizarre forms in their dreams. I just added two plus two to come to my conclusions. One might just wonder, "Did Jesus speak in parables for several reasons?" This is the basis of our study.

Not only did Jesus speak in parables while He walked on this earth, but God also has often used parables and/or metaphors in His explanations. In the book of Jeremiah, for instance, God was just getting Jeremiah started in his work, and then this occurred:

> *The word of the Lord came to me again: "What do you see?" "I see a boiling pot, tilting away from the north," I answered. The Lord said to me," from the north disaster will be poured out on all who live in the land."*

> (Jer. 1:13–14)

As you will see here and continue to note in our studies, God speaks to us on many occasions using parables. This is why our dreams, *most of the time*, do not make (earthly) sense to us. God is indeed speaking to us in our dreams and in many cases, in those same types of parables.

This is nothing new, you know. About this time, some of my readers might be saying, "If God wanted us to know this, He would have explained this to us in His Word." My opinion is that He did. We just didn't catch it, and if we did at one time, we didn't hold on to it.

When I first felt God was (still) speaking to us in our dreams, I naturally got very excited! I also felt a little hesitant and maybe even a bit afraid to take such a bold step of faith to share this. I had a great blessing to share, but I also had a lot to lose if I was wrong.

> *Not many of you should presume to be teachers, my brothers, because you know that you who teach will be judged more strictly.*

> (James 3:1)

I prayed very hard about this book for some time before making the decision to write my transcripts. I prayed for direction *every* single day during the entire writing process. This decision came through prayer and fasting. I've taken my diaries and some of my many dreams (over the years) then made a choice to publish this study. As I prayed, here is just one answer God gave me in a dream. I will share quite a few of them with you in the main dream chapter.

While praying and asking God whether I should take this leap of faith and write this book, I had this dream: I was driving on a highway, and the ocean was immediately on my right side. The water was so close to me that if I drove any closer to the right, I would have been in the ocean. There were very tall buildings to my left, but they were at an angle and leaning in my direction. I would say they were leaning toward me at about a thirty-degree angle. The buildings seemed to be hovering over a portion of my car and looking as if they would fall and smash upon me at any moment. I knew by driving on this road I was taking a risk, but I drove down the street in faith.

When I awoke, I immediately felt this dream had to do with the faith I was asking for. In fact, the dream isn't too hard to interpret even on the surface. To drive that road took faith, and again it was faith I was praying about.

Let me share something with you here, folks; writing a book is not all that glamorous. First of all, the contents of this book border on a subject that is very hard to tie directly into Scripture. Then there's the trouble of having a book published. And last, but indeed not least, is the fear of whether it is truly in God's will. My questions during my studies naturally were: *Is this happening only to me? Should I share my discoveries and experiences from God with others? Is He telling me to write this? And could this be happening to others too?* As I prayed for guidance, many times I got really discouraged, but then He gave me the dreams of encouragement I needed to go on.

That same night in which I had the dream of driving along the ocean with the buildings leaning into me, I also had a second dream. I dreamt about houses that were built in the trees. The houses were being balanced in these trees, and my wife and I (as well as others living in the trees) would enter our home with faith that these homes would not fall out of the trees. As I entered my home in the trees, it was solid and sturdy, but I would look down and be fearful that the house would not hold or stay firm within the trees. I became more confident with each passing day that I lived within the trees. Through time and faith, I lived comfortably in the trees and learned to feel secure as time passed.

When I woke, I felt this dream had to do with what I was praying about. There is not much to explain to you, is there? The dream almost speaks for itself. And in a way, that dream had to do with your dreams too. That is why I mentioned it was not only I who lived in these trees (that took faith) but others too. And if you noticed, as time went on, I became more and more faithful and confident in my new home.

When you read your Bible, especially in the area of dreaming, please take note of two things. One is that dreams were sometimes interpreted by a second person and in *every* instance, only by men of God. Daniel and Joseph were two men of God who were able to do this. The other thing that became apparent to me as I studied was that men who were not of God *were the only ones who needed the interpreting.* All of God's people awoke knowing their own dreams! When God came to many of His people, He came to them in visions and dreams. There is not one record of a man of God needing an interpretation. Not one! When the other Joseph, Mary's husband, and others we will study later, had dreams, they all awoke to action; never slumbering, never hesitating, and never doubting. The next important thing we will discover is that those who had a dream who were worshipers of God never needed an interpreter. God was their interpreter!

Studying the Bible will be the *only* way to get a full understanding of what I am explaining. I want people to wake up and not just take my words here in this book. Study these things for yourself and the truth will set you free.

There is one thing the Bible does not truly explain, and that is *how many* dreams came to the people. The Bible, in general, only explains small portions of many people's lives, but never do we get an entire life history of any one person. It is my opinion that we have not been privy to each person's one and only dream. I believe these people had many dreams from God and the Bible only gives us specific examples for our review.

The Bible also shares with us the words, "He had a dream," but it doesn't specifically tell us if the dream was or was not in parable form. *But* the dreams that we do read about and that are explained in detail are usually in parables! Were some of those dreams direct words from God, or did Joseph (for instance) know to take Mary and Jesus to Egypt by understanding a parable dream? Were some of those dreams visits by angels? Were they delivered in parables, as we discussed here, or were they straight commands? One thing is for certain: each and every person knew his or her dream came from God!

Please don't be afraid to read and study the Christian Bible. It is not as hard as some people make it out to be. God would never have written words that common man could not understand. R.C. Sproul, in his book *Knowing Scripture*, says, "What kind of a god would reveal His love and redemption in terms so technical and concepts so profound that only an elite corps of professional scholars could understand them?"[1]

---

[1]   R. C. Sproul, *Knowing Scripture.*

Well put, R. C.! I am an avid reader and I highly recommend this book *Knowing Scripture.* There is one thing to be said, folks, and that is, if you think reading the Bible is hard, then indeed you need to plant yourself in a strong Christian church and let God open your eyes, because once He lifts the veil from your eyes, all truth is seen in His words. What was hard one day comes into light the next. I think that's another of God's ways of assuring you that you have been saved. One day it was gibberish and then only one day later it all makes sense.

Before we move on, I want to share another initial fear I had in preparing this book: knowing crooked people would come forward and attempt to make financial gain by saying, *"Call us on our **hotline** and we will explain your dreams."* For me, a man who loves the Lord with all his heart, soul, and mind, this was a very deep concern. Again I have to say, it took a lot of prayer as well as a tug from God to convince me to go on with the writing of this book. Please hear these words, and in humbleness and prayer I will tell you, stay away from such talk! If God is talking to you, He will let you know what He is saying! You do not need any interpreter, including me, to tell you what God said to you. We do not have a God of confusion! We will cover more of this in the chapter, "How to Interpret Your Dreams."

Let the prophet who has a dream tell his dream …

(Jer. 23:28a)

CHAPTER 2

Remembering Your Dreams

This was the dream, and now we will interpret it to the king.

(Dan. 2:36)

To begin with, you don't need to be taught how to dream; we all dream. But what I'm going to share with you are the ways to remember your dreams. Our goal here, then, is to pull your dream(s) *out* from when you are asleep and place them from, let's say, one part of your brain into another. Not knowing a thing about the anatomy of the brain but speaking as a simple layman, I just know I need to take something out of here and put it into there. We forget our dreams, but we surely remember what we had for dinner yesterday. *That's* the place I want your dreams to be transferred to. Get it? Now let's learn.

Let me explain this analogy to you: I look at our brains as supercomputers. Have you ever noticed if a person is knocked unconscious, the medical staff (or paramedics) ask, "What year is this?" or "Who is the president of the United States?" Why do you think they do that? Because a brain is nothing more than a fantastic computer, storing information constantly, so when it gets turned *completely off,* it needs to reboot. As it reboots, our brains search for *all* the memories, statistics, and other things they've stored and places them back into categories or even folders. Our brains are indeed like our home computers. They store information. Everything is there; we just need to find it!

The first important thing I need to warn you about is this: if you're married, your spouse better know that you are about to become a bit of a pest; just ask my wife. She has had to tolerate me, as well as to learn to adjust to my dream life. Sometimes I even speak out loud when I'm asleep and dreaming. Occasionally I will verbalize, in a rather loud voice (in the middle of the night), "Praise the Lord" because the dream I just had was just snatched from my subconscious and into my conscious (if that's what it is?). Therefore (and briefly) in my conscious state and with exuberance, I will praise Him and go back to sleep, *excited* and looking for more. (Note I didn't say I wrote it down; I've moved past that stage. I've simply grabbed that dream from one part of my brain and stored in the place where I remember what I had for dinner last night.)

Okay, the second-most-important thing you need is to take a notepad and pen to bed with you. You will probably need a little lamp or flashlight too. I use one of those clip-on lights—the kind you might use while reading a book in bed. I clip it onto my yellow pad (and clipboard) with a couple of pens handy, and now I'm ready. I don't like it when my pen runs out of ink, and at two or three in the morning I tend to tolerate it even less! If you are one who needs glasses, make those handy as well. Okay, now you've got your tools; you're ready to go!

After my first two years of writing down dreams, my wife got this brainstorm. She bought me a tiny recorder, so sometimes I'd use that instead of the pen and paper. I would wake from my sleep, push the record button, and speak my dream. This tape recorder works much faster, but I've got to admit, when you're writing down your dreams, you tend to waken just a little more, and the dream (sort of) reveals itself as you are writing. The more time you take in your conscious state, the better, for as you know, the time it takes to *write* takes longer than talking into a recorder, so I'm not sure I'd recommend a recorder in the beginning. I consider myself a professional at this, I guess. What's a professional dreamer? Who knows? Lots of practice I guess. Sounds good though!

Next, be patient! In fact, pray for patience because you can't always expect results right away or even every night. However, some of you (of course) will, but some won't. How to *interpret* your dreams and other important lessons will be discussed in later chapters, and they are going to come easy compared to this. Remembering dreams from a state of deep sleep to an alert state of consciousness is in itself a sort of art, so this is the most challenging thing we will need to accomplish.

You'd better understand something else too; there will be times when you will only remember parts of your dream(s), and sometimes you will need the entire dream to get an interpretation of it. I still wake up, even today, with only a part of the dream in my memory. So what do I do? Not a thing. I praise God that He allowed me to remember even part of my dream, and I don't worry about it at all.

Don't forget who's in charge here—God! When you pray and ask Him for His guidance when it comes to your dreams, then you need to just wait on the Lord. It *will* come. "He is faithful and just …" (1 John 1:9). Plus, you've got to realize that He wants to communicate to you, *maybe more than you'll ever know.* To this day, after years upon years of prayer and practice, I still go through occasional dry spells. For whatever reason God has, it just happens.

I have often wondered why I'd go through dry spells. Then I came to realize that He's always in control, and whatever it is, maybe He's just got nothing to say to me today. Or maybe He just wants me to let *you* know that we all go through this. I often go weeks without anything special coming from God, but I don't worry or shed a tear because I trust Him! He'll find me when He wants me.

I also want you to recognize that many dreams are no more than just simple dreams. They don't have to all be messages from God. For instance, let's say that I had a dream about my grandson, Nicholas. In my dream, Nick and I spent the day at the beach. Maybe we eat a hot dog, make a sand castle, and then surf a little in the water. When I wake up, I don't go looking for some deep meaning to that dream. It was what it was: a day at the beach. Then another time I might wake with a deeper, more bizarre dream—one with deep meaning. By the way, we will discuss our dreams that have *deep* meaning a little later. The whole point is this:

> **Do not be anxious about anything, but in everything, by prayer and petition, with thanksgiving, present your request to God.**

> (Phil. 4:6, emphasis mine)

When you dream, you *must* be able to write down that dream just as fast as you can. This is very important, friends! In fact, this may be the actual key to success. This is why as *soon* as you wake up, you must write down that dream—and not just when you wake up in the morning. Even if you wake in the middle of the night, you must write them down.

In my beginning stages, I'd awaken in the middle of the night and (first) try to go to the restroom and write down my dream when I got back into bed. *Big mistake*! Hold it (if you can). As the dream comes to you, and as soon as you are able, get up off that pillow and write down whatever you remember. Even if it's only a small part of the dream, write it down. Through practice and diligence, your patience will pay off. Then get back to that pillow just as fast as you can. Don't dilly-dally around with anything. No snacks, no TV, no checking text messages. Hit the hay, and get back to sleep. You will most likely have another good dream that same night, and potentially, you'll be able to write down yet another dream (or maybe even two) before the night is over.

As you begin to write, more will come to you, I promise. You just start writing *whatever* you remember and … Well, what I do is sorta say, "C'mon, c'mon now, give it to me, Lord," and it just comes! It's fun—it really is!

Don't ask me why, but here's something else I have found to be true. When it rains, it pours, and when it's dry, it's really dry. Don't mess up a good opportunity by getting up and turning on Jay Leno. Get back to sleep and get dreaming again.

After you have practiced this for a time, you'll be able to remember dreams more easily. You will actually begin to develop sort of a habit (or a skill) for remembering them. Count on it! Remember this: when you practice *anything* long enough, you will improve, no matter what that is. I consider this gift as sort of an art; with practice, it just gets better and better. I've remembered as many as four different dreams in one night, and that's without waking to write them down. In fact, if I remembered four dreams, I might have forgotten a few more that same night.

"Wait a minute, you said write them down right away," you might be saying. You're right, I did say that, but I've done this for so long, I've had more dreams than you'd ever, ever imagine. I've learned now not to necessarily write them down. I've actually developed a skill of staying asleep and even changing dreams. It's like turning the page of a book (or a channel of the TV), and then I write them all down in the morning. I have also developed and trained myself to wake up (if I want) and then go *right* back to sleep again *to that same dream*! To me, this is the coolest thing!

I can actually wake myself almost anytime I want during the night. In my dream, when I am ready, I pull myself out of a sleep, make my notes, and then go back to the pillow. I have trained part of my brain to always be aware that I am studying as well as sleeping, dreaming, and even praying. I even wake up at night and find myself (or part of my brain?) singing praises to the Lord or simply praising Him at *the same time* as I am dreaming. It's like one part of me is singing and praising Him while another part of me is dreaming, and yet another part of me is taking notes and waiting to wake me. Whew, exhausting, isn't it? Not really, it's great! It's fun. I actually and truly believe God is a very special friend to me, and I think He's *loving this.*

Some of God's best messages have come to me during naps. Maybe it's because we don't really go into a deep sleep when we nap. It could be because of the light in the room or even the noises outside, but we are actually lighter sleepers when we nap. Waking and writing down dreams seems a little easier when I nap. I don't often get a chance to nap, but when the opportunity arises, the results have been a blessing.

I've also found that napping in a car will give me nice dreams too. Let's say we're on a road trip and Shar's driving. I'll doze off and get some really great dreams. God knows it's a good time to communicate with me; I just close my eyes and allow Him to give me something to praise Him about.

One of my *all-time* favorite dreams was while I was napping. This dream didn't come in a parable either. Every time I write about it here in this book or tell the story aloud, it brings tears to my eyes.

One day I was dozing off to take a nap; I was in my bed on top of the covers. In my light sleep, I began talking to God. I was looking up toward the sky, and I asked, "Where are you, God? I look for you and I can't find you. Lord, where are you at?" He answered, "Right here, Manuel … I'm always right here." I heard a voice, but I couldn't see where it was coming from, so I asked Him again, "Where, Lord? I can't see You; where are You?" He said, "Right here."

As I looked up (in my dream, remember), I saw a rip in the air, at about ten feet above my head and to my right. Another example (for the best mental picture) would be a person standing behind a curtain, on a stage. His hand slowly came out of this rip, but I didn't see His face, or maybe it was that I didn't remember the face. But I know the Bible says, "Nobody has ever seen the face of God" (Ex. 33:23). I knew nobody had ever seen His face, and I surely wasn't expecting to be the first. Anyway, the voice repeated to me, "I'm right here, Manuel, and *I'm always right here.*"

I then looked back up at this slice in the air that produced his hand and watched it slowly go back into wherever it came from. There were no clouds, mind you, just a different dimension, if you will. It was like there was a rip in the air. And then (here comes the best part) again, in a very, very slow and in quiet, peaceful voice, He said, "I'm right here, Manuel, I'm always right here." The second time He said that, He didn't put His hand out, but I knew He was there.

Note: Today I live my life *every day* trusting He's just right there! When I look up to pray to Him today, I don't look up toward the heavens—I look ten feet and to the right. He's right there! Then all of a sudden I heard my grandson, Nicholas (then five years old; he's eighteen today) come into the house, and I awoke from my nap. By the time he reached my bedroom, yelling, "Papo," I was writing my notes with tears in my eyes. I couldn't even see the paper.

And here's another really cool thing; nobody calls me Manuel. It *is* my given name, but I go Manny … to everybody, I guess but God!

It seems the more I develop this awareness of God, the more tears flow from my eyes. Stop and think about this, and put yourself in this wonderful position (and you soon will). *How chilling!* I am absolutely convinced God is speaking to me, folks. I want to honestly say that *He wants to talk to you too.* I believe this with everything I hold true, and yes, what a chill.

When you make your notes, you are going to discover that you will not always remember every detail of every dream. Never, I repeat, *never* get frustrated. Would He want you to? We are talking about a loving and patient God. We are talking about a God who allowed His people to remain in Egypt for four hundred years. He then walked His people through the desert for forty more years. Jesus Himself walked in the desert for forty days without food or water while He prayed to the Father and prepared for His ministry. Moses wasn't even used by God until he was well along in years. This is how *our* God works in *our* lives, sometimes slowly and with great patience.

You had better realize before you start that you're going to get to His way of thinking and not yours. Do not rush Him or get frustrated at Him. If you don't remember your dreams, think of Joseph and all the years he spent preparing his people. God works for the good for those who love Him.

Some of you are going to find the results of remembering dreams will occur quicker than others. More than likely this could mean that you probably remember your dreams more often anyway, especially the unusual ones. So if you're the person who already remembers many of your dreams, then half of this training course (or at least this chapter) will indeed go much easier for you. The next step then for you will be found in chapter 4, how to interpret those dreams. But hey, that doesn't mean skip chapter 3; we've got more good stuff to come.

Some dreams will come to you in a simple form, and others will be more complicated. I have found that the ones with the deepest meanings are the ones that seem to come in a type of parable. It seems like my most bizarre dreams are the ones with the deepest meanings or messages. I don't know why; it just is what it is.

Also, it is important for you to understand God's love for you. When Jesus died on the cross, He died for you and me equally. God doesn't think in terms that Billy Graham, Charles Stanley, or Chuck Smith (or anyone else, for that matter) are any better than you and me. Remember when I grumped earlier about people calling us hypocrites? Well the point is, we are all sinners, and we all have the same opportunity to have a relationship with Jesus Christ. He died once for all. He didn't die for Billy, Charles, and Chuck, and then later die for you. He died once and gives us an opportunity to know Him *now* and then someday in heaven. So if you are taking in this study privately or maybe with a friend, your spouse, or even a Sunday school class, remember this: some of you will find results faster than others.

Some people remember Scripture faster than others, right? But we are all the same in God's eyes. *It's not God's love for you that is a factor here.* He loves you more than you will ever comprehend. This dream study has to do with training, patience, and prayer. God will speak to you in your dreams, so please *don't* be in a hurry!

My oldest daughter, Christina, studied the deepest subjects in the area of mathematics when she was in college. How she does it, I'll never know (and mind you, I'm a numbers person myself). She's taken classes in college that I've never even heard about. To say that she's a mathematics major would be cutting her short. The skills she has placed into her studies are incredible. Now if I studied with her, or even right beside her, she is going to arrive at a formula *way* before I do. In fact, I might get frustrated a little, but I must understand that we are all built differently. Have you heard the saying, "Be patient, God isn't finished with me yet"? Well that fits this! The solution to the math problem will be there for both Christina and me. It might just take me a little longer. God wants you to remember your dreams just as much as He wants me to remember mine. Be patient, be praying, and be calm. It will come.

Generally speaking I believe I remember my dreams more than most people, of course. The secret is, you must practice to remember dreams, whether from God or not. It is this writing practice that makes you ready for the big one. Even now, there are days when I'm not even sure if I dreamed or not. I've read the dream studies say we dream every night. How they figure that, I'll never know, but let's say we do. Then I don't know if I do or not. Even after all these years, I don't know the brain and how it works. I'm a simple man who loves God and has studied His Word for many years; I am *far* from perfect. God just opened a door for me—a door that all of us have had our entire lives.

I guess He just made a decision to allow me the honor and privilege of learning and now to share and teach it to others. In fact, these are my thoughts on what's going on in the world, for what it's worth. The end days are coming soon and are in many ways already here. His Word says that in end times we will "have visions and dream dreams." I think He is using me to make more people aware of these dreams so they will occur naturally. The Holy Spirit has been alive and well since He hovered over the oceans even before Genesis 1. Yet we seem to have become more "in tune," and He, the Holy Spirit has revealed Himself boldly in both the twentieth and twenty-first centuries. At no other time in the history of the world has the Holy Spirit been as active as these two time periods as just after Jesus went into heaven … and *now*!

Now let's get back to the study and learn how to remember your dreams. When you begin to wake up, you *must* try and grasp the dream *as you are waking.*

You are indeed conscious of the fact that you're *trying* to find God (in this way), so He is going to help you. Remember to pray and ask God to guide you and help you. When you begin to wake, think hard about what you may have dreamed about.

If, in this slumber, you are not remembering, then start to scan or search your mind. Now pay attention! This is the secret: What you are attempting to do in this state of slumber is to search for something that will take hold and help you to remember the actual dream (or the rest of the dream) you had. You are looking for one simple thing, anything, and then everything will begin to come back to you from that starting point—that starting point that I just called "something."

For instance, when I *start* to wake up and don't remember my dream, I *immediately* start thinking like this: *Mountains, water, houses, birds, my family, work, swimming, crying, furniture, cars, driving, surfing, hotels, friends, airplanes, cutting the grass* ... I look for *anything* that might trigger the rest of my dream to begin coming back to me. There are a ton of things that can trigger that starting point of my memory. I usually start with things that mean something *to me*. In other words, I don't think of snow skiing, because I don't snow ski. I don't think of parachutes because I don't skydive or scuba dive or camp. But what I am doing is scanning or scrolling anything that will trigger my memory to find my dream and then move it into *my* consciousness *and it works* ... hey, it works, believe me. You'll snag that one thing and then another will pop and another and the dream will unfold!

Do you remember earlier in this chapter when I mentioned our brains are nothing more than supercomputers? Well, have you ever done a search on your computer for a word or a group of words? You place that word into your search engine, and away that computer goes. And if you watch it, it simply goes flickering about as fast as the eye can see. What is it looking for? It's looking to *grab* onto that word you asked it to, and then the rest of the document appears. Like I said earlier, and I think you knew this already, our brains are nothing more than supercomputers, so scroll and search.

Remembering your dreams is *so* close to what I just described that I can't give you a better description. Now remember, some of you wake daily and remember many of your dreams; this is not necessarily for you. This *search* thing is for those who say they never remember their dreams. You've got to trust me here. You simply must start searching (or scanning) as you begin to wake. When you catch that word, you'll just about laugh 'cause *that* word *will trigger* the dream, and then you'll see, it will all appear.

Let's say the memory is that of a tree. Then (in my mind) it'll go something like this: "Oh yeah, the tree had a swing … and oh, oh, under the swing were dogs trying to bite my toes … Oh my God, and when I stopped swinging, they didn't really want my toes, they just wanted to play with me." As you write, God will assist you in moving the dream into the other part of your brain where you remember easier. As you write, it'll come back to you. And as you write, you might even begin to cry because you're going to be so happy. And that's how it works, guys! But don't stop here; there's so much more:

This system of hunting down and searching my memory indeed works. Of course it does not always work 100 percent of the time, but many times it surely does. In fact, nothing works all the time, right? But when it works correctly, this is what happens in my brain. Let's say I am doing this scanning/searching and the trigger word, person, or thing comes to mind. Let's say it's a fence. That key word becomes a trigger and flashes a sequence of events that causes the dream to piece itself together. And pretty quickly too, I might add. This, too, takes time and practice. But it's going to come, you guys, so don't get discouraged. It's gonna come!

When beginning on this fantastic experience, you must develop a twenty-four-hour conscious awareness that you are a part of your own study on dreams. It's as if you must keep yourself psyched up and in prayer to get a full commitment to remembering your dreams. By doing this *all day long*, your mind is training itself to be alert and aware of the memory process of your dreams. Then, when you begin to awaken, you'll realize that you are in this *mode of awareness*. In other words, if you wake up and then go to the restroom, or first pour a bowl of cereal and *then* try and think about your dream, chances are it will be too late. You may not have the same result as if you would have started this process during your waking slumber. At the first sign of waking is when you are in this state of semi-conscious awareness and you will get your mind on the right track.

Think of it like this, too; it works for me. Have you ever woken up on the day you were to go on some fantastic vacation? In your morning slumber, before you even give that last stretch in bed, you know you're headed for a great time somewhere on vacation. It's your first thought of the day, and in fact, before the day even gets started, that is what's on your mind. That same type of awareness is necessary here too. *You must get your brain in gear to remember to remember.*

Oh, here's another thing many can relate to. Many reading this have been into sports; let's just take boxing, just because. You know way ahead of time that you're preparing for this big fight (or big game). All day, every day, part of your mind is simply focused and psyched on this main event. The same goes for this study. You've simply *got to* get fired up and let God know, "I'm determined. Lord, I want this. Please bless me with dreams; I want to know You even more."

Now remember, dreaming is something we all do. This is no new thing. It simply goes without saying. Dreams are something we have always had, and it's a part of our natural makeup, from the beginning of time.

Now if I remember correctly (from my childhood), I learned somewhere that a dream only lasts for a second or a millisecond. I had to think hard on that during my study, and here's my conclusion. I thought carefully about this, and to those who think dreams last only a second, I say, "Bologna!"

But ya know what? I'm going to let them have this one and not argue with science. I'm going to concede and say that the actual dream might take just a fraction of a second. In conclusion I say, okay, so my dream occurs like a flash of lightning. Well, my God can take it from there and move it, shape it, or expand on it around in my head anyway He wants to—and that, my friends, is that!

So whether the scientists and doctors are right or wrong and our dreams last for an hour or a second makes no difference to me. It's the process of events taking place in my brain during my time of sleep. Whether it is before or after the dream that God is working out in my head, I don't know, and frankly, I don't care. He's talking to me (us), and I'm going to prove it to all of you.

Well, we'd better get to the next chapter. It has to do with skeptics, and well, we'd just better get to it. Plus I need to address the skeptics before I get to the next important chapter after that, "How to Interpret Your Dreams." Let's deal with the skepticism and negative thoughts that might be going on in some of your heads. If I lose a few of you in the next chapter, it's your loss. Believe me, it is indeed your loss. Those who finish this book and then practice it and do their own study with their dreams, God *will* talk to you!

CHAPTER 3

To All the Skeptics

Before we start this chapter, I think you should know I'm probably my own worst critic. Not only am I a student of Christianity, but I am a teacher of God's Word, and that makes me *highly* accountable for what I teach. Now that in itself makes everything I do and everything I teach very important. I have an obligation as a teacher (and a Christian) to stay within the boundaries God has set before me. As a teacher, I have to deal with all kinds of cautions, tests, and affirmations before I open my mouth to teach.

When I teach, and this is what I am doing here, I must do so with incredible research, confidence, and guidance from the Holy Spirit. It was this type of caution, as well as much research and many affirmations from God, that brought me to the place I am at today. I had to be 100 percent sure it was the Holy Spirit leading me to teach this very special subject. You might say I felt my head was in a noose. One mistake, one slipup, and off goes my head ... well, sorta; at least I want to be that cautious about this!

Over the years, I've studied the various types of religions as well as the various branches of the Christian faith. I've also studied cults and groups not associated with the Christian faith. As part of a prerequisite and training for being a good teacher, I found that solid preparation was necessary before entering the classroom. Josh McDowell wrote a book called *A Ready Defense.* I read that along with Bruce Bickel and Stan Jantz's book *Guide to God* and Richard Warren's book *Answers to Life's Difficult Questions.* Oh, I can't forget *Give me an Answer* by Cliffe Kenchtle. These are just some of the hundreds of books I felt were great books written by good Christian men. I've listened to Calvary Chapel (KWAVE) radio for years upon years, including the program, "Pastor's Perspective," to make sure I, too, can answer questions asked of the hosts. You might say I participate, or let's say practice my answers when I listen to that special hour of Q&A.

You see, to be a good teacher, one must always be prepared to give an answer for the glory that is before us. A teacher should live life that way, you know. In my library of Christian and study books, I have read hundreds of books to better prepare myself as a teacher. I even enjoy some of the older classics like those written by C. S. Lewis and others. I look at being a teacher as similar to serving in the national guard. As good Christians, we are always to be *on guard* and *ready for service.* Having a teaching position or sharing the Bible with others is a study that must be done every day of a man's life. It is a lifetime of devotion to God and His kingdom.

I also believe a good Christian must stay on constant guard because of what we do. What do we do? We sort of guard the Word. I keep books in my library such as, *The Encyclopedia of Bible Difficulties* by Gleason L. Archer, or *Unger's Bible Handbook, Halley's Bible Handbook, an Expository Dictionary,* and many more study guides ready and accessible at all times. Also, when someone takes on the true and important duties of a teacher, one must do so with faith, with confidence, and with a deep sense of conviction of the responsibility held before us. I believe it's the Holy Spirit who is the teacher, and I am only the vessel He speaks through.

During the many, many years I've spent on this book, I looked for any kind of sign(s) that gave me an out, but instead, I just obtained repeated messages to go on. Was I actually hoping for an out from writing the book? Of course not, but I wanted to be absolutely sure it was God's book and not mine.

First and foremost these messages and dreams came to me through many years of studying the Word of God. Then, through my dreams, which I am sure are from the Lord, came my works. And most important of all were all the prayers and my relationship with God that was put into this study. The heaviest and most earth-shaking of all was watching Him work through *other people's dreams*. You see, you may have thought I was going to give you a long and boring chapter affirming my dreams, but not so fast mate. What I'm about to share, however, chilled Shar and I more than anything and everything combined.

You see, during this study, dozens upon dozens of people shared their dreams with me, and *none of them* had any knowledge or idea that I was writing a book. Was it nothing short of the world's biggest coincidence, or was the hand of God guiding people to share their dreams with me? Over these countless years, an incredible number of people came to me to share their dreams *and* in the oddest places. All the while, only Shar and I looking into each other's eyes and knew that God was working in all of it.

At times, I would walk away in tears, knowing the person who just shared their dream with me had no idea that I had been at this for years, writing my manuscript. And I was looking for, and needing, confirmations and affirmations that only He could have given to me. It was and is more chilling than I could ever, ever describe here on paper. The oddest people and the most unlikely circumstances would surround these testimonies of dreams. God was directing every bit of my life!

As I shared earlier, at the time of these writings, Shar and I were the only two people on this planet who knew about this book. Yet, over and over, day in and day out, we would be somewhere when someone out of the clear blue sky would start a conversation by saying, "*I had this crazy dream last night.*" And then the next thing, suddenly they'd be sharing with us their dream. I would always look over at Shar and give her a wink, as she would look back at me and smile. All this time, we both knew, "This is indeed the hand of God."

Now, one might at this point say, "We all have people tell us their dreams." And, I agree—people do share their dreams, but I'm not finished yet. Funny thing about God, He made sure He put His signature on His work! I would get phone calls from the oddest people—people I hadn't spoken to in years. They would call me to say hello, ask how we were, and then share how things were going in their life. Then, within that conversation, a story about a dream of theirs would come up. This happened so many times. Was this a coincidence, maybe? But it sure helped to support that this was God's way of confirming His presence. It was all those odd happenstances that kept encouraging *my* fears and doubts. And though I believe and trust in God, I'm still human, I am still a bit afraid … *and I am a cautious teacher.* I had to continue to test, and I was not yet fully convinced, even yet.

Now, even greater than the fact that nobody knew I was writing a book was this: are you ready? *Nobody,* but nobody, except my wife, knew that I was even studying my own dreams and dreams in general. Not a soul on this planet knew about my diaries and the years I had put into this. Not my father, Manuel, not my pastor, not my children and not my coworkers. *Nobody*! So here we were with neighbors, pastors, relatives, people at church (even some I hardly knew), strangers, and friends, some whom I see often and others I hardly see at all. So many people shared their dreams, not knowing for one instant, *with not a clue,* that I'm on a mission.

As I stated, nobody knew I was writing a *book.* Then I shared with you that nobody but Shar knew I had been even studying dreams. I want you to understand there is a difference between the two. When people shared their dreams, it wasn't because of my manuscripts *or* because of a study; they had no clue! I also mentioned that I believed God's signature was all over these sharing of dreams. Let's look at some of them and you tell me: coincidence or God.

One day, while visiting my family in Ohio, we were all getting up after a meal at the table. This was several years ago, when I was truly searching for signs from God. You folks reading this just have to understand this. I just *had* to know that this wasn't me. I just had to hear/see God not only in *my* dreams, but I needed affirmation in other places too.

So my father woke up and came into the kitchen to have breakfast. While he was eating his breakfast, he looked up at me and said, "I had this crazy dream last night," and he proceeded to tell us his dream. I then asked him why he thought his dream was so crazy. His answer: "First of all, I *never* remember my dreams; that's what makes it really crazy." Then I looked over to his wife, Isa, and said, "How many times can you remember my dad sharing a dream with you?" She thought for a moment and said, "In all our years of marriage [twenty], this is a first." I looked over at Shar, smiled, and winked. Only she and I knew chances are only God could have wanted this to happen this way. Notice I said, "Chances are." I'm not done yet.

Then one day we were attending church on Sunday morning because we had just moved from Canton, Ohio, to Virginia Beach, Virginia. As we arrived at church, we found out a substitute preacher was on the pulpit that day. The regular pastor had taken ill the night before and called whoever pastors call when they get sick. We lived very near Pat Robertson's *700 Club*, but we attended a neat little church near the water called Beachlawn Baptist. Well, this visiting pastor was at the pulpit and said, "I had this message prepared for today. In fact, I have been writing this message for several weeks, but I had such an odd dream last night. I think I want to talk about it and share my dream with you people instead." So was this a mere coincidence? Okay, maybe I'll give you that one too, but I've got more, so be prepared.

Hey, listen, I'm going to convince you. I simply did not want to write this book unless He knocked me over with a stick, but ya know what? He used a baseball bat instead.

One day I was praying for the household of a neighboring couple. These people (who were very dear to us and had been married a very long time) were fighting ad bickering constantly. In fact, they were speaking of getting a divorce, and it bothered me quite a bit because I love them both dearly. That night I prayed and asked God, "Should I intercede and get involved in their problem or just pray and stand back?" That was my prayer; this was my dream.

There were about one hundred people all on ladders. They were painting the outside of the top floor(s) of this tall building; each person was at the top of their own ladder. The foreman of the crew was up on top of the building, pacing back and forth on the roof, looking down on the workers and instructing them while they were painting. I was on the ground looking up and watching the foreman orchestrate these painters with such choreographic precision that I was in awe.

Every stroke of the brush was done in sync with each other person, one next to the other. As far as my eye could see, I saw these people all painting with such accuracy; it was an amazing sight to see. Then all of a sudden two of the workers fell to the ground, and I looked up at the foreman; I motioned to him that I was about to help the two who had fallen. The foreman yelled down to me, "Don't touch them, they have to learn the way. I will teach them. You are not to interfere with them when they fall. They must learn. They are mine to teach as I please."

So I stood back and kept my distance. When I woke, I was immediately taken back. Naturally I felt this dream meant for me to stand aside and not get involved in our neighbors' troubles. I continued to pray for them, and within a couple of days they had worked through their problem, and to this day they are happy and married. The message to me was that God would work it out.

Okay, now comes the best part of this story. That same morning, about one hour after I had gotten out of bed, our daughters, Christina and Kelly, were outside on the patio with us having a morning cup of coffee. Both daughters were visiting us from out of town (we were now living in Wildomar, California). Now Nick, my grandson, was only five years old at the time, and he was last to rise that morning. He woke up, came out to the patio, and immediately said, "Papo, I had a weird dream last night. Do you want me to tell you about it?" Remember, Christina, Kelly, and Nick knew nothing about my work. So I said to Nicholas, "Yes, Nick, tell us your dream." (Note: He had never shared a dream with me prior to this day.) I had prayed that the night before about the family problem I mentioned. And after having my own dream (which I was all excited about), I anxiously asked Nick to tell me his dream.

He said, "We were all in this big boat going through some deep water." I interrupted him to ask him, "Who all was in the boat?" He said, "Lots of people, including our family." He proceeded, "When we were in the boat, there were these people I don't know. Then two of them fell into the water and we thought they were going to drown. Papo, you jumped up to help them, but the Captain of the boat yelled at you and said, 'Don't touch them, they will be all right.'" Nick continued to explain that after the two went into the water, they also went *through* the water, but then there was clean and fresh air on the other side of the water!

I asked Nicholas to further explain what he meant by that. He then gestured with his hands. "Here is the water, and there is the air above the water, where the boat was, and under the water there was air too." His hands were describing a body of water with air on both sides of the water. In other words, the water was in the middle, so there was air above and below this body of water.

Now think about this, folks. Could the water have been the trial of these two people who fell into it? Could God have spoken to me through Nicholas, explaining and confirming *again* to keep away from this family's problem because He had everything under control and after a little while, the couple would find air again? Could it be? Who knows for sure? One thing is for certain; being the critic that I was, my first question was, "Why did they keep going deeper down and not rise back up where the air was supposed to be?" Was God saying we must go deeper and deeper in some of our own problems, and He doesn't bring us out of our problems the same way we go into them? Was God saying, "In your world the air is up, and when I'm controlling things, the air is where I say it is." (Funny.)

Again, who knows? One thing I did know was that I truly was convinced that Nick's dream worked hand in hand with mine. More than that, I felt convinced it was a second and confirming answer to one prayer. I shared with my wife later in the day that Nick and I sort of had the same dream. In my mind's eye, it *was* the same dream. They were about two separate incidents where two people were in trouble. Two people needed help, and both times I was not allowed to reach out and interfere. This incident not only helped me to confirm my nonphysical involvement with this family's marriage, but it also helped put one more mark of evidence that God was working on me and this book.

Okay, now some of you might be saying, "Well, your interpretation is your own. I might have seen that dream in an entirely different light." *Again, I'll agree.* You *might* see a different message there. I won't argue with that for a minute, but they are *my* dreams.

God is working in my life and that is part of the principal teachings of this book. God works in all of our lives, but differently, and only you know your own dreams. And if He uses someone else, like Nicholas, his dream was actually meant and directed toward me, not Nicholas. In my dreams, and the way I wake up and write them down, are the results I see or analyze the first thing in the morning. God sort of tells me—or should I say the first thing that pops in my head—what I *know* God is telling me to listen to. Don't ponder the thought. Don't write down ten or twenty different "what ifs." Just take God at His first words and go with it. It has worked for me time after time.

This is why it is so critical that you understand there will not be too many dream interpreters out there. In the Bible, God's people effectively interpreted their own dreams. *In every instance*, it was only those who didn't know God who needed help. I will fairly warn you, don't fall into the trap of someone else telling you what your dream was all about. God put the dream there; He will also give you its meaning.

Most of the time the only way I am actually able to interpret another person's dream is if I know just about everything there is to know about that person. If you are a stranger and I do not know what is going on in your life, how in the world can I tell you what God has in mind when He speaks to you in *your* dreams? We will cover this more in the next chapter, "How to Interpret Your Dreams."

On the day our church had a visiting pastor, this was the dream he shared. Funny thing is, I didn't know this man, but in this particular case, I felt like I knew what his dream meant or should I say, I concurred with what he thought it meant.

In the pastor's dream, he was sitting on his front porch watching the cars go by. His house was located at an intersection where there was a four-way stop sign. The cars were driving very fast, and not many of them were paying attention, not stopping at the intersection. In fact, he explained, some didn't even slow down. He was very afraid there would be an accident and people would be gravely hurt. He would get up off his chair and occasionally yell out a warning, but the cars would not stop. They continued to drive without yielding to the *stop sign*. He said he would run out to the intersection and yell, scream, and wave his hands to try and get people to stop, but they would not.

Here is what he saw in that dream. The cars represented people he encountered while being a pastor. The stop signs represented his desire to stop people in their everyday lives and share the Word of God. His desire to witness was reflected in those cars driving by his house (his life), and his love for them was expressed by holding out his hands and yelling for them to stop. His deepest desire was for the cars to stop and hear him preach the Word of God and be saved. In his anxiousness and zeal, he would rise from his rocking chair on the porch and yell at the cars—like maybe every day of his life.

As I mentioned earlier, I didn't know this man and it is not often I hear a dream from a stranger, and can interpret that particular dream. In fact, I don't even try. I'm not here to interpret dreams, only to teach you how *you* are to learn to listen to God. A very dear friend of mine named Jan Sayer would share dreams with me now and then. I never once was able to understand any of her dreams, but I didn't know her well enough (then) to have even been able to try. I have had my sisters, Kathy and Michelle, share their dreams with me, and I understood them, fully. Of course they didn't know I was doing this dream study either. We will discuss my sisters' dreams in a later chapter.

> **In the very same way, these dreamers pollute their own bodies, reject authority and slander celestial beings.**
>
> (Jude 8)

> **And afterward, I will pour out my Spirit on all people. Your sons and daughters will prophesy, your old men will dream dreams, your young men will see visions.**
>
> (Joel 2:28)

So have I perhaps convinced my readers in this short chapter? I can't really answer that. To those who don't really know God or can't read my heart in these pages, there will never be enough proof. But truly, friends, I started the first line of this chapter sharing with you that I am my worst critic. I, too, am so obedient to God's will I would shudder in fear if I was teaching something new. Greg Laurie, an incredible pastor and evangelist says, "If it's new it's not true, and if it's true it's not new." Wow, how cool is that!

A true and loving student of God knows the Spirit of God. A true and loving teacher of God's Word knows to walk lightly and be careful of every conversation.

CHAPTER 4

How to Interpret Your Dreams

In a dream, in a vision of the night, when deep sleep falls on men as they slumber in their beds, he may speak in their ears and terrify them with warning.

(Job 33:15–16)

"If it's new, it's not true … and if it's true, it's not new." That's a quote from one of my favorite pastors, Greg Laurie, founder and lecturer of the GREAT Harvest Crusades.

May God bless speakers and pastors all over the world who serve in radio ministries. Chuck Smith, Greg Laurie, David Rosales, David T. Moore, David Jeremiah, Raul Rees, and so many more—who can count all who have given their lives over to the ministry of Jesus? I encourage you to pray for all the men and women in and behind the scenes at the Calvary Satellite Network as well as other radio ministries around the globe. Once again, may God richly bless you. Your work has blessed thousands of lives, including mine. I pray for you all every day, from those who answer the phones to those who clean the studios at night. Thank you!

If you don't spend time listening to Christian radio, you ought to! The strength and teachings I receive from listening to these many radio stations is worth more than gold. Please, do me a simple favor.

Stop right now, in the middle of your reading, and pray for radio ministries; they affect so many lives around the world.

The reason I used Greg's quote at the beginning of the chapter is that it's right on. If someone comes along and tries to say he has something new that God has revealed to him, *run away.* Don't walk, don't think twice—run for your life. **Nothing** God does in a Christian's life will be new. His words were written long ago, never to be updated, never to be amended (with the times), never to be added to. No new revelation will ever be given to you or to me or to some man who says God told him the world is going to end on a certain date. Simply stated, God's not going to start to reveal Himself in any new way.

When the Christians of the 1960s were baptized into the Pentecostal movement, many conservative Christians went into shock. It seemed all of a sudden a new generation of people were speaking in tongues. Was it new, or did we stop using some of the gift revealed to us generations ago?

Some referred to it as the Neo or New Pentecostal Movement, but was it really new? Of course not! I've read that it was in the mid-1960s and that the Azusa Street Mission in Los Angeles was where a part of the rebirth of speaking in tongues may have begun ... or maybe I should say it was there that the Holy Spirit came down upon the people. It soon spread to the (mighty) Pentecostal and Assemblies of God Churches. Before we knew it, the Holy Spirit had again brought Pentecost to the Christian people of this end-times generation.

When God speaks to people in their dreams, that's not new either. It may not have been as recognized as back in the day, just as healing, speaking in tongues, and prophecy were not always recognized, but those gifts haven't disappeared either. Maybe they have been forgotten or even tossed aside. The Holy Spirit never took away any of His gifts.

In fact, we might say they were simply unused for a season. But did any of those gifts just disappear? Some say yes; some say no way.

Gifts of the Spirit are not new, are they? And Jesus' teachings or speaking to us in parables (in the Bible) is also nothing new. When you read the Synoptic Gospels (Matthew, Mark, and Luke) look for a couple of things. The first thing is that Jesus told many stories in parables. Matthew 13 and 20 through 22 are good examples of this. Mark 4 and 12 are two more good chapters to study parables. Then Luke 8, 12, 14–16, and 18 are also just a few more chapters all filled with parables told by Jesus. And it is those types of parables that will be helpful as we untangle our dream interpretation(s).

Another important study you will find in both the Old and New Testaments is *God spoke to many people in dreams.* This happened so many times *and* to so many people that one must wonder why we stopped addressing it. Another thing that needs mentioning again is that God spoke to His followers as well as nonfollowers, or believers and nonbelievers.

He spoke in dreams to both the Jew and the non-Jew. We see from the Bible's example that God can and does speak to anyone who hears His voice. This is why I mentioned several times already that I believe God speaks to every single person in the world in dreams. It is in the listening and knowing how to hear His voice, in our dreams that are the keys. Now let's learn how to listen for Him.

The first and *most important* thing is this: *you will interpret your own dreams!* Well, in a way … God will actually reveal the interpretation to you. Yes, I've already crammed this down your throat; well, you're going to have to listen to me here again and maybe even again later. Why? Because it's important! Do not allow phony psychics to utilize this for profit. Yes, a dream can be interpreted by another person, just like tongues are interpreted by another. You must really be close or intimate in that person's life to be able to assist her in her interpretation. Let me give you an example why.

My sister, Kathy, had a dream she shared with me. Like I've mentioned earlier, many people, unbeknownst to them, have contributed to my book. Shar and I have not only been astonished at the countless number of people who share their dreams with us, but we have looked at it as a direct sign from God. Again why? Because, as I said before, *nobody* knows about my studies but my Shar. Yet it seems so often, more frequently than a mere coincidence, that dreams are shared with me time and time again. In fact, it's rather spooky, actually. This is just another sign from God instructing me to write.

So, can I interpret a dream? Only if I know the person really well. Now let me explain, so let's get back to the story and the dream from my sister Kathy. She called me one day from Canton, Ohio. Canton is my hometown and the great pro football Hall of Fame city. Kathy told me she had a really bizarre dream and wanted to share it with me. It's funny how people always seem to say their dreams are either crazy or bizarre.

Here was her dream. She was fishing in a small boat and a much-larger boat started coming toward her. Kathy said she was frightened of this large boat as it headed in her direction. She reeled in her fishing line and started speeding off in the small boat (that she was piloting), but this larger boat was gaining on her in pursuit. She kept looking over her shoulder, noticing that the big boat was gaining on her, but she throttled down trying to outrun it. As she made every attempt to outrun this large boat, she simply could not. It was much bigger and stronger than her little boat. She explained to me, "I felt a pull. It was like I felt I wanted to be on that large boat, yet I was deathly afraid of it."

She continued to share that chase scene with me and I do not, even today, remember who won the chase. But tell me, folks, what was this dream about? Do you know? Unless you knew my sister, how could you dare guess?

My explanation is this. If you don't know Kathy and just about everything in her life, how on earth can you interpret her dream? You see, this is *my* sister; I know her well, so I shared Kathy's dream with my wife after I got off the phone. Until the day she reads this book, she won't even know she's in here. Here is the interpretation of Kathy's dream. First of all, Kathy is a fisherman from the word, go. She loves to fish and finds peace and comfort in her fishing. At the time she owned two boats, I think one for small lakes and one for larger lakes. She and her husband had been separated and in fact were probably in the midst of getting divorced. Kathy's husband is a giant of a man, so he represented the big boat. She, a small four-foot-eleven woman, represents the small boat.

I truly believe her dream was this: She felt urges to get on the big boat while it was chasing her, yet she was scared, just like she had urges to try and hold onto her marriage yet she was fearful of it as well. Kathy's desire to run from the boat *and* run from her marriage were one and the same. He's a big man; he was the big boat. She's a tiny gal; she was the small boat. Her pull to get on that big boat is nothing more than the hurt and pain one goes through when contemplating a divorce. Should I stay, or should I go? She wanted to be with the big boat but felt safer in the small boat. Today Kathy is divorced; you might say she stayed in the small boat.

Was that simple to interpret? If you knew Kathy and the things surrounding her life, then yes, maybe it is easy to interpret a dream. But of course one must be aware of how to interpret dreams as well. The first key to interpreting your dreams is this: In most cases, God is going to make your dream comparable to the things currently surrounding your life. And like I said earlier, most of my good dreams come in parables, so look beyond the black and white; ask—simply ask—God to reveal the dream to you!

So you want to look for the dream, and characters in your dream, to represent things happening in your life. Forget those books that tell you if you're a bird in your dream, then you have always wanted to fly a plane. *Again*, scrap those books; in my opinion, I've proved them wrong in *every* case I've studied. Not once did they hold true. I have read, and own, almost every book written on dreams and what they are supposed mean. They belong in the fireplace. There are books on dreams that you look up, let's say a pink elephant, and that's supposed to mean you desire to eat ice cream (I just made that up, but you get my point). *Hog wash!*

Before we go further, I guess I'm going to repeat something. One of the fears I've had while writing this book are the false wannabes. Let's call them prophets or dream interpreters. My concern is that soon eight hundred numbers will crop up and look to make financial gain from dream interpretations; will it be yet another dreamers' hotline? *Please* don't get taken in by them.

> *I have heard what the prophets say who prophesy lies in My name. They say, I had a dream! I had a dream! How long will this continue in the hearts of these lying prophets, who prophesy the delusions of their own minds? They think the dreams they tell one another will make my people forget my name, just as their fathers forgot my name through Baal worship. Let the prophet who has a dream tell his dream, but let the one who has my word speak it faithfully. For what has straw to do with grain, declares the Lord ... "Indeed I am against those who prophesy dreams," declares the Lord.*
>
> (Jer. 23:25–32)

The key to interpret your dreams lies between *you and God*. I'm going to share something with you now, and I will probably repeat this a few times in this book. *As soon as I wake up and write down my dream, God is giving me the interpretation—at the same time I am writing down the dream.* I have never—not once—had to stop and deeply think about the dream from the night before. So I never had to contemplate it while, let's say, eating breakfast. I've not looked to someone else or even given it a second thought. God has always been right there and answered His own servant. *Even before it's fully written in my diary, He has given me its meaning.*

Now sure, I've had to think about the dream. Remember in chapter 2 that I taught you to scroll your memories trying to remember the dream. Then one thing pops up, you write it down and then another part of the dream comes to mind. *That* happens all the time, but almost at the *very* moment I start to write it, God will trigger something in my mind that makes me 100 percent sure that's what He's telling me. Man, how exciting!

In the book *Good Morning, Holy Spirit*, the author, pastor, and disciple of the Lord, Benny Hinn, speaks of several dreams. One of those dreams was from his mother, Constandi Hinn. She had a dream involving a half-dozen roses. When she woke up from her dream, those roses were no longer flowers but her children. Now think about this. She looked at what sort of represented the number six in her life and instantly knew what God was speaking to her about.

Mrs. Hinn didn't go anywhere to have this dream interpreted. She didn't have to ask a neighbor, nor did she find need to call a hotline. In fact, she didn't even consult her own husband. Constandi Hinn knew instantly that her dream was from the Lord, and she knew its meaning. No interpreters, no sideshows—it was between her and God.

Remember earlier I mentioned I wasn't the kind of guy to go camping, nor am I a fisherman. When I have my dreams and seek the Lord for an interpretation, I only look to those things that are in my life, let's say my world. And Mrs. Hinn—well, her dream had six roses. She woke and just *knew* she had six children. It simply fit!

Benny, in this same book, also explains several dreams he had himself. He explains about the dream where he was led down a set of stairs. It was in the dark, and he was chained to two prisoners. As he descended into this dark chasm, he later awakened. Benny never mentioned being afraid, and in fact, in two of his dreams, he knew immediately that they were from God.

I am here to tell you that we all have these dreams, and we must *learn from them.* Let's study some more so we can learn to interpret what God is trying to tell us. From there we grow deeper in Christ by reading the Bible, praying, and looking for Him to speak *to us* in our dreams.

He's there, so look for Him. Search Him out, and He will sup with you. *Hey,* you can trust me on this one: God wants this relationship with you; you've just got to find Him (now) in your sleep.

The most important part of this communication with God is to start by writing your dreams down. Your dream diaries will become very important to you. It will be the tool necessary for the *development* of interpreting. If you simply wake, think about your dream, and then go about your day, you will never get off first base. You must grow and develop your mind to understand that this will be a daily part of your life. Then writing down your dreams will become a habit. From that habit, your brain will kick in and start remembering even better because you're logging your dreams in the diary. This diary will be the beginning, and *God* will expand it from there! Remember again, practice makes perfect. Practice anything and you'll get better at it. Some of you will get this right away and some won't, but don't get discouraged; *practice.* Hey, God's not gonna give up on you, so don't *you* give up on yourself either.

Now let's take a minute and talk about the diaries themselves. My diary isn't exactly the kind you would buy for your teenage daughter. What I mostly use are spiral notebooks and/or a yellow legal pad. I don't have a pink diary with a lockbox on the outside, that's for sure. On the right side of the page, I write down the dream. On the left side of the page, I write down its interpretation, if I receive one. Hey, I don't always remember my dreams, and if my dream has to do with going to the beach with my grandson, Nicholas, then I write that in there too. I don't try to read into that. The thing is, make it a habit to *write down every single dream.*

Some mornings I only remember (maybe) one little, simple thing about the dream. I write that down even though I don't remember anything else. *Why?* Practice makes perfect! So you see, I write down everything, even if it's only for the sake of recording it. There are times when the left side of the page (or column) remains blank. There is no interpretation. A day at the beach is a day at the beach.

In the early stages of my dream research, I thought I might dream something, only to come back a week or two later and find its interpretation, like wrapping up an unsolved mystery. That never happened, not once! He has yet to give me a dream where I found its answer at a later date.

So, after writing down years of dreams and after praying about this my entire adult life, I have found God, then, to be both the author and interpreter of my dreams. You will get no help from any outside influence. His faithful *one* on *One* relationship is all that is needed.

So the solution or formula for interpreting dreams is relatively simple. You dream your own dreams, right? Then He gives you the results or interpretation. The training relies solely on practice and prayer. Practice remembering your dream is a very important formula, but the key word is practice. Practice makes (close to) perfect. You must write them down as soon as you can and then, pray, meditate, and just wait on God.

You just need to get started with this in your life, and you can surely count on God to be there. *Don't ever forget this: He wants a relationship with everyone.* I truly believe this from everything I've ever learned. And since God has a different outlook on time than we do, He's got all the time in the world for you. He waits for, hopes for, and counts on a relationship with each and every person out there—*you too!* He wants our prayers as well as our adoration and companionship.

Let me share with you what I'll call a little secret; I live each day thinking that it's only God and me. Now that doesn't mean I'm so naïve that I don't think you're out there too. What I do know is *everyone* is important to God. Give God your time, and He'll give you His. And since His time is not our time, *man* do we score when we have a relationship with Him.

I tell Shar, "In God's eyes, I'm Adam and you're Eve." God has nobody on earth today that He'd rather spend the day with than His Adam and Eve. After all, that's the way He started life down here on earth. So Shar is Eve and I am Adam … and as far as I'm concerned, He's got all the time in the world to hope that I care about Him, love Him, pray to Him, and make Him my God.

By the way, you can do this too. Don't ever think God is so busy He has no time for you. *All He has is time,* for both my life and your life. God's got all the time in the world to give to each of us. My pretend thought of being Adam and Eve just means that I don't look at the world as being *so* big that God doesn't have time for each of us. I look at the world through God's eyes as being so tiny that *each* of us can be His Adam and Eve. Live that way! Think that way! Know that you are very special to Him, and *nothing* would make God happier than for you to realize how special *you* are to Him. Hey, I just *know* this! Don't go through this life without the joy I'm sharing with you here. I'm an only child to God … but *you are too.*

Now let's get back to dreams. The way I figure it is this: I've been dreaming for years. I remember some of those dreams, and others I don't remember. Some days I'd wake afraid of a nightmare, and other times my dreams would be rather pleasant. But it wasn't until my first bus driver dream that I described earlier that the doors of my mind flew wide open and dreams became more than something that occurs only when I sleep. Today I live my life where my nighttime is as important to me as the hours I am awake. My dream life is as important as my day life.

Although this has become a very important part of my life, praying still comes first, and then, of course, studying God's Word. Next is fellowship with God's family, who are the people at my church and other Christians. These are all first priorities and prerequisites to sleeping and dreaming. This dreaming thing has become the icing on the cake. Nothing has changed in my life when it comes to reading God's Word or anything else. For those of you who really love the Lord, look at the bright side: now you can worship twenty-four/seven.

Here's the way I look at my life: In the day, I pray and study the Word of God. At night, I pray and wait on God. Win-win.

Then one day I got to thinking: *Is this why some people have re-occurring dreams? Is God trying to say, "Resolve this issue and/or discover this dream and then we'll move on to the next?"* After all these years, my answer is unequivocally *yes*. This is *exactly* why we repeat our dreams or even nightmares. We haven't resolved the lesson or issue being conveyed by God. Or might it be that at one time it was simply a nice dream, and later it has turned into a recurring nightmare?

If I had a dream that I was swimming in a pool and a toy boat was following behind me, it might be fun or funny. Allow that dream to recur over and over again, and sooner or later it becomes a nightmare. I would actually become afraid of a simple toy boat if it kept chasing me night after night.

I've discovered that once God has given me a dream and I recognize His message, He moves on to the next dream. "No need to repeat it," is what I feel He's trying to say to me. *"Did you get my message?"* (And He knows if I did.) *"Well then, let's move on,"* He might say. By the way, we will talk more about this in the chapter, "My God, Why Can't I Sleep?"

I am going to share some of my dreams with you in the chapters to follow. I am doing this so you will look at not only my dreams but the circumstances that surrounded my life at that time. I want you to see the analyzing process I discovered in regard to dreams.

I think there will be plenty out there who will be skeptics. But then again, just say the sky is blue and some people will argue with you. However, I hope everything will be plain to see. There will be no mystery behind my dreams.

Some might say, "Well, you were having a dream about drowning because you were taking swimming lessons," for example. I'm going to expect that from some of you, and there will be no puzzle to what and how I am going to explain my dream and the process regarding them. Everything God has given to me He has kept simple and I have no doubt many of my dreams come from Him.

Today my prayer is that He opens your eyes to your dreams, just as Jesus explained to His disciples the meaning of the parables after giving them. When you first read that parable, even you might not have completely understood it. Then, after Jesus explained it to you, your eyes were opened—or at least I hope they were. If they were not, then you would fall into those of whom Jesus said, "They were ever seeing, but not understanding." But for those who follow the teaching of Jesus, I have *no doubt* you will rejoice over these teachings and your personal experiences with our Lord and Savior.

> **Yet when I preach the gospel, I cannot boast, for I am compelled to preach (teach). Woe to me if I do not preach the gospel!**
>
> (1 Cor. 9:16)

61

CHAPTER 5

Getting to the Heart of the Matter

A word was secretly brought to me, my ears got a whisper of it. Amid disquieting dreams In the night, when sleep falls on man.

(Job 4:12–13)

It is time to share some of the dreams I have experienced since beginning my journey. I share these dreams only to give you a firsthand look at all the work, as well as all the trials and errors I went through over many, many years. I do not share these dreams because I want you to know my life, per se, but to teach you the things that occurred to me. I hope that you can take a faster train to our ultimate destination: to have a deeper and more wonderful relationship with the Father.

I keep several different diaries at the same time. I keep one on my nightstand, one on my bookshelf in my library, and yet another on the desk in my office. As I explained to you in chapter 2, remembering the dreams will be the hardest thing to do. One should keep a pad handy, next to the bed, for quick notes. Understanding your dreams, praying prior to going to sleep, asking God for guidance in your study, and even keeping a sharp pencil are all tasks that need to be done to fulfill this destination of getting these dreams from God. Waking up and remembering the dreams will be the hardest part of your study. Always be prepared and patient. *It will come.*

After writing down and studying my dreams for these many years, it became easier and easier to remember them as time went on. After all the training, I now find I can wake up and go right back to sleep, remembering two or three dreams in a night without writing them down until morning. But as they say on TV, "Don't try this at home." Through all of my experience and training, I have trained my mind to store my dreams in some sort of vault in my head. I found myself using less of the pen and paper at night and waiting until morning to log them into my diary. Then, as I mentioned previously, Shar bought me a recorder, so sometimes I use that instead. But before that, I would get up in the morning, and the first thing I would do is go to my study or the kitchen table, pull out one of my diaries, and write down my night's dreams—all of them! Whether I had one, two, or more, I would write them down once I woke for the day.

There were several times when I went through long dry spells. I examined every part of my life and even worried about it at times. But He was faithful and came back to me, and I never got discouraged or lost patience. Although nothing changed (i.e., marriage, health, kids, job, finances and other things like that), I sort of concluded that the culprit was my lack of memory. For some reason, I went through spells where I knew I had dreamed, but I could not remember any of the dreams. Once I went almost four months without remembering a dream. My memory of recalling my dreams had, let's say, gone to the desert. It was like things were going really well for me, and then they didn't. Later things would go really well again, and then they wouldn't. For the life of me, I couldn't figure out why my memory had taken a vacation or whatever. I would then go back to basics and take out those diaries above my headboard (rather than at my desk), attach that light gizmo, and started writing once again throughout the middle of the night. And even after doing that, I went through weeks of rarely remembering a dream. I often wondered, "Am I losing all I achieved? Is it all over? Is God telling me that this book, and all I have put into it, might not be what He wants of me?"

Then I thought maybe I wasn't eating right. Maybe I wasn't thinking right, or maybe I had even left the right fellowship with God. Maybe I changed the way I prayed. Was I making a mistake in what I was trying to accomplish? Maybe this wasn't meant to be. All these doubts and more were running through my mind. After all, I had dedicated so much of my life to this project. I was honestly very concerned.

As I had all these thoughts running through my head, I had to ask God what to do. I prayed, "God, don't fail me now." But as time passed and I learned to grow in Him as well as have patience, I learned that this was *all* part of the lesson. As Charles Stanley once taught me in one of his great messages, "God, what is Your goal for this trial in my life?" Through prayer, patience, and listening to the still voice of God, I concluded, and not in a dream, that we all can go through periods of being in a desert. The desert has always represented a time of trial and testing. A desert doesn't have to be a place; it can be a thing: dry periods of praying, maybe a period in your life where you just don't want to go to church or read your Bible. It is this travel through the wilderness (desert) that builds our character. God hadn't deserted me. It was all part of the growth He wanted to put me through so I could come out sharp as iron and ready to teach *you*.

So here I am, the teacher and studier of dreams. Yet I was worried that I, too, might have my dry wells. But then that well sprung up again to give me the living water. Don't be discouraged if this happens to you; it happened to me too.

Many years ago, I went through a period of my life where I all but abandoned the Lord. Some call it backsliding, some say even meaner things, but I just wasn't worshipping as sincerely as in prior days, and I realized it too. Business opportunities came my way, but I passed them up, not feeling God was as near to me as in times past. We chose some wrong paths, and with that comes hard times as well. Satan tempted me by bringing these bad deals across my table. Instead of turning them down, I became tempted by profits, so I bit!

I grew up in the '60s and finished school in 1973. I went to two high schools, James Madison in San Diego, California and Canton McKinley in Canton, Ohio. Although I did pretty well in school, drugs were prevalent in California during those years, and I was one of those who fell into the trap. Later I became saved (1972), but I was still tempted by my addictions. As I grew older, and as a weak man, I fell back into the trap. I thought I was a mature Christian at twenty-two, but I was no different than a young child. I needed guidance, but my guide and mentor had died and left me. She went to be with the Lord at the age of forty-one. She was my mother, Helen.

I attended church as a young man and even taught Sunday school. My mother brought me up knowing the Lord, reading His Word, and praying regularly. Then that first restaurant/bar deal passed my desk, and the money, at my young age, overcame me. Sad, isn't it? It's hard to look back on life's mistakes.

When I was a young boy, I grew up in an Orthodox home. My mother was a Greek Orthodox, and we attended Holy Trinity in Canton, Ohio. We worshipped in a Greek Orthodox church. To this day, I am very proud of that. As I grew older, my mother found more of what she was looking for in a Baptist Church, so when I was in about the tenth grade of high school, we started to attend Scott Memorial Baptist Church in San Diego, California. After joining the Baptist church, I immediately noticed that the Word of God was studied with more determination than when I attended Sunday school at the Orthodox Church. I think, to me, the Orthodox group read the Bible with more reverence. The Baptist church taught me how to hold that book in my hands on a daily basis and live with it near my heart at all times.

As I grew older and became a more mature Christian, I indeed noticed a *huge* difference between the weekly liturgy of the Orthodox and Catholics compared to the Protestant churches, who indwell and really study the Word of God. Although I occasionally visit a Greek Orthodox church now and then, I always notice that not much has changed. Again, I'm very proud to be half Greek and to have been raised in the Greek church. But can anybody really learn and grow when the same service is being repeated week after week, month after month, year after year? How can anybody learn what God wants out of his or her life without getting to know God on a personal basis and asking the Holy Spirit to teach him or her daily? Now, again, please don't take me wrong. I'm very proud of being Greek, Spanish, and Italian, but all three of those cultures rely on repetition in their weekly worship, and I like the *meat* taught at traditional Christian churches. It's the truth we should all seek, not our heritage. Just because my Papo (grandfather) brought me up one way doesn't mean that I don't have the choice and desire to want to be fed, and to the fullest. I thank my mother for breaking that chain and expanding our worship to a new horizon.

During my teenage days, while I was attending high school in San Diego and partying with my friends, I was also studying the Bible to suit my mother's requests. She sort of insisted on it. The Baptists are pretty good with a mid-week Bible study, and my mother always had two or three a week in our home as well. Even a few of my drug-using friends came to some of my mother's Bible studies. And ya know somethin' funny? A few even accepted the Lord. Although I wasn't a very good Christian in those days, my mother was putting a lot of good things into my mind. It might not have reached my heart at that point, but the seed was planted. I thank God that I had a mother who never gave up on me.

The years went by as my father, Manuel, my two sisters, Kathy and Michelle, my wife, Shar, and my two daughters, Christina and Kelly put up with a really bad cocaine habit: mine. It took many years and a whole lot of prayers before I came to realize that I needed Jesus fully and not just part time in my life. One night, after many years without drugs, before going to sleep I asked God why I had to go through all of those drug years. Was I saying He did that to me? Of course not! But what I was looking for was a miracle from Him. I didn't want to struggle over drugs all those years, and I never understood why I had to put myself and my family through all of that. I just wanted the Lord Jesus to bail me out. Cocaine is an evil drug, but so are all drugs.

I thank God *every day* that it is all behind me now, all except the prayers. Because of my past, I find myself praying for drug addicts and people locked up in jails and prison *every single day*. I have always had a least one pen pal in a prison to keep that person company during the hard times when he is down. I was there, I felt the pain, and I sort of owe it to them. I learned from that experience, and now I use the good and bad knowledge in my testimony.

A dream I had one time was that I was in a garden and these snakes kept attaching themselves to me. They would release their venom into me and I would get really sick, but I would not die. I had that same dream a few more times but only with more and more snakes. Every time I dreamt this, more of them would attach themselves to me. I was just covered with snakes, all hanging on to me, with their fangs embedded into my body. The first time I was bit, it affected me greatly and made me very weak and sick. Then, the more times the snakes bit me, the more immune I became to their venom. When they would attach their fangs onto my arm, the snakes would dangle. I would take in the venom and get weak and eventually fall to the ground. As the future dreams progressed and these same snakes continued to bite me, I would end up not being affected by the venom. I would simply shake off the snakes from my arm and in a loud voice say to the snakes, "You can't hurt me anymore."

I related this dream to my cocaine days and the help I was trying to give to others around me at that time in my life. The snake, of course, was Satan and/or the demons associated with cocaine. The cocaine itself was the poison and one I could not shake off. But as time went on and the drug left my life, I was able to use my old habit to strengthen others. The Lord turned around my habit and all the bad and gross things that went with it. He helped me to shake off the poison and now use my weakness to strengthen and witness to others. Now I can say to people, "If you need help, come talk with me; I've been there. I've shaken the snakes from my arms." Praise God!

Another dream I had, I was inside a war zone. I was allies with the Mexican Army. Some group or groups of others were shooting at them and killing them in cold blood. For some reason, this Mexican Army was unarmed, I guess. People were dying all around me, when suddenly I looked up and saw my wife. She was behind a chain-link fence and was safe from harm. I didn't know why she was safe. After all, chain link is not armor, but she was there and safe from harm. All of us who were trying to defend ourselves in this war could see that inside this chain-link fence, in the middle of the war zone, Shar (and others) appeared safe.

When I woke up, I pictured the fence as being inside of God's family, and she was in the safety of salvation. That war was being fought all around her, but she was safe from harm. The fact that I was outside the fence only represented, to me, the continuous battles I face every day attempting to lead others to get inside the fence (fellowship with God). I didn't, at any time in my dream, feel threatened myself since I was outside the fence. But the one I loved most, my wife, was in the secure and safe arms of my Lord and Savior, and that is exactly where I needed her to be. As soon as I awoke, that was my thought of what the dream meant, and I accept that!

I thought about not using that dream in this book. Do you wanna know why I did? One can look at that particular simple dream and respond, "Well, there's a farfetched story. That fence could have been anything." You're right! It *could* have been anything. But it turned out, I put that dream in to better express that when I wake up and God gives me a quick interpretation, I am convinced it is correct and it is from God. Some of the dreams to follow will be more complex yet easier to understand. That one there above needed my own explanation of God's opening of the interpretation.

My wife and I have always enjoyed the sport of football. Maybe it's because I come from Canton, Ohio. I think it's in your blood when you're from Canton! But man do we get into the game! Shar loves the Minnesota Vikings and I like several teams, but dem Browns are my dogs. We, as a couple, like football a lot, and *I've got to thank God* for that. Amen.

There were many times in the past when we would frequent our neighborhood sports lounges and watch the game. While there, we would have a few cocktails or maybe a few cold beers, and those drinks and the surroundings seemed to spruce up the game. I wasn't walking real close to God at that time, so I didn't care much about my witness. But it seemed that conversations about God will always seem to crop up, and although I wanted to pop in and say, "I know that answer," I never could because I had ruined my witness. I hated those days, especially because I really love the Lord, yet I messed up a lot.

Can you imagine what it would feel like to be a doctor and to see an accident occur in front of your eyes, yet not be able to respond? Can you imagine being a college professor of a prestigious university and bump into a group of your students who have always honored and respected you, yet you're just a bit sloshed? Not only that, but even if you wanted to enter the conversation, the alcohol's got you so bad that night that you couldn't get into a conversation if you tried. Well, those are some quick examples of how I felt when these things happened to me. I once lost three students in my Sunday school class because I was found drinking in a country western bar. Was it wrong? I'm not going to judge, even myself, but to ruin my testimony and have them disappointed in me—that was the part that was wrong.

I had a dream where I was having some cocktails with Shar. In fact, we went into this same bar about two or three times within the same dream (in and out). My daughter Kelly was calling me on the telephone with an emergency. She would say to me, "Dad, come quickly, I need your help." But at the same time, I had been drinking. I couldn't drive because I had consumed enough alcohol that I couldn't drive my car, so I ran. Every time I got to Kelly, it was too late to help her. I never remembered why she called, but that doesn't matter. The point was, whatever reason my daughter called was important enough to run to her aid and help her, but I couldn't; I was always late.

I have to address, once more, the skeptics, doubters, and maybe even the psychologists too. You might now be saying, "Well, your guilty conscience from consuming alcohol affected you to the point that you were having these dreams." On the surface, and thinking from another point of view, those answers look pretty logical. But after years of having dreams and studying them, I've concluded this is God's way of talking to us. You look at my dreams as my subconscious mind reflecting my dreams, but as I look at them and say God is dealing with *all of my life through my dreams*. This is the purpose of this entire book! I choose to look at my dreams as spiritual, as you have the right to say they are simply the result of my current environment. In fact, you will be able to (probably) rationalize absolutely everything in this book if you want to look at it from a worldly position, but it is for this reason that I have come forward. I think it is more than our subconscious minds working with us; I think it is God working in us!

Let us look at a much deeper dream. Hang on, this one has twists.

I was at a place where a lady was guarding an ancient twenty-four-karat gold statue or some type of golden idol. It may have even been a gold doll. Inside of it were what she called "holy ashes." She kept telling me that these ashes were never to be disturbed. "Whoever disturbs these ashes will be forever cursed," she would say. She repeated these words over and over as she chanted these words to me. Curious, I opened the container to take a look at the ashes inside. Some of them suddenly spilled on the floor. I sort of laughed in disbelief as I put the top back on and went about my merry way. As I went on with my life, days later, I felt this evil spirit tugging away at my pants legs, constantly pulling at me. Although I could not see this evil spirit, nevertheless, it kept tugging and pulling at my pants leg. As I tried to progress or move forward in my life, this thing kept tugging harder and harder, attempting to stop me from moving even a few inches forward. In this dream, I battled this evil spirit every day, although I could not see it. I finally got really mad and rebuked it to leave me alone. (I often look back and wonder what took me so long to react.)

This dream immediately represented, specifically, these following interpretations. The twenty-four-karat gold statue, or whatever it was, represented life. The ashes were my life's faults, shortcomings, screw-ups, and mistakes I had made. It seemed I was afraid to go on in my life because of them. I felt guilty about my past, my drug years, and all the mistakes I made as a husband, son, and father. I could no longer do good things in my life because of this guilt. The pulling and tugging on my pants leg was Satan constantly reminding me to feel guilty about all my mistakes and that I could never serve God adequately. The Devil was pulling me down and trying to convince me I could never make up enough to please God, so I should give it up.

This dream really hit home and was very real to me. So did its interpretation. I hope you can see the stories and background I gave you at the beginning of this chapter so you will better understand me, where I'm coming from, and things like that. Now I want you to see how God dealt with me through those dreams, and again, I'm going to say it: He's dealing with you too, so listen.

Jesus died once for all (Rom. 5:8), and that death and resurrection covered our sins *for those who accept Jesus as their personal Savior.* I'm not the first person to have been saved as a young teen (or child) and then turn my back and walk away from Him for a season. For me to return someday as the Prodigal Son (Luke 15:11–32) is not an excuse, though many use that story's example. But the story itself shows Christians have also blown it many times in our lives. Yet, the Father is there with open arms when we return. I will never forget that my mother trained up her child in the way he should go, and my return to faith is a promise of God. Thank You, Lord. In the story of the Prodigal Son, Jesus explains to us the rejoicing that went on when this man's son finally came home. Paul says the angels in heaven rejoice over one sinner when he turns from his ways ( ). And again, Paul tells us to look ahead (Phil. 3:13) and forget what is behind us.

When I finally did rebuke the tugging this demon had on me, it was actually *me telling Satan* that I finally woke up. I realized that I would never have been able to come to God unless Jesus, His Son, died for me at Calvary. So in my dream, as I awoke, I looked at this as a sign to press on, move forward, and work hard for the Lord. I was not to ever look back and wait for an instant sanctification, but through Jesus, I had already been made righteous. From that day forward, I no longer had that dream. It is the Holy Spirit of the Godhead who delivers these dreams to us. This is another important part of the lesson, folks. The Holy Spirit is not a Ghost. He's a He!

I'm going to tell you once again that the most important factor for interpreting your dream is that *as soon* as I wake up, the answers to my dreams are the first thing to come to my mind. This is how I look at the results. I do not wait until later in the day, think it through, or go over it with a shrink, a neighbor, or even my wife. It is *my first* impression of my first interpretation that the Holy Spirit gives to me. These are His answers and this is my faith, so that is what I look to find.

I want to share this: Slow down! My future success needs to be gained through a process of one step at a time. There are no shortcuts. I can never get to my destination unless I wait on the Lord. One more side note: Many people come to me with multilevel marketing ideas. Along with being an entrepreneur, I've spent <u>thirty seven years</u> doing accounting work. I work for other businessmen and women and take care of their books and taxes. In all my years, I've never found an easy way to make money at these businesses. They're hard work and take all your dedication.

By the way, folks, in my life and in my mind, success is not a financial thing. It is maturity, spiritual wisdom, and knowledge of the Word. *That* is my success—to every man give an answer to hope that is in you. Always be prepared to represent the Lord. Stand ready and armed. That is the number-one level of success that I both pursue and desire.

I look at this life as standing in a batter's box. We swing and warm up until God calls us in the game, always ready, always prepared, yet never knowing when you'll get put into the game. Although you think you're next up at bat, the coach can take you out of that box at a moment's notice or allow you to swing away. I also look at the Christian life as if I'm in a job interview. It may last ninety years, but it is only one long interview. I've got to make every word out of my mouth count. I have to always be prepared to give the Boss an answer as to why I did this or that and then He'll place me either upstairs or downstairs. Eternity is a curious thing. When is it ever going to end? Am I saying that I don't care about making a good living and taking care of my family? No way. But "Seek ye first the kingdom of God and His righteousness, *then* all these things shall be added unto you."

Let's go to another dream. I had an invoice in my hand, and I was on my way to go and collect this money due to me from an individual. It seemed my destination was a five-star restaurant. This restaurant was so high-class and top-graded that it had a two-week waiting list just to dine there. I walked in, and there were three owners behind a counter. I handed them my bill, and they looked at me and smiled. They reached under the counter and handed me their bill. I looked at them with fear and surprise. I didn't remember whose bill was higher, but I was a little afraid because I wasn't expecting them to pull out a bill for me.

The dream is simple enough. Now let's look at what came to mind when I woke up. The bill I was holding to collect on were the good deeds I had done in my life. With a smile of arrogance on my face, I entered the restaurant, which represented heaven. The three men, may be the Trinity or maybe they were just three men. When I went inside with this goofy smile on my face, they reached under that counter and handed me my bill. On that paper was a list of all the bad things I had done in my life. (Uh-oh!)

I looked at this dream with a little bit of curiosity. Being a Christian, I already know I'm not going into heaven with a list of good deeds! Man is that ever a scary thought! I know it will be Jesus and only Jesus who pays my debt in full. I still had that dream and wanted to share it with you.

Here is yet another dream. I was in a garage dismantling an automobile. (By the way, I know very little about cars.) As I was taking this car apart in pieces, I wanted to donate all the parts to charity. As I took each part away from the body of the car, I handed them over to the charity group one piece (part) at a time. In my dream, I found myself hiding or trying to hold back two pieces of the car for myself. I didn't want to give them up. I kept these two pieces hidden from the charity, and I simply didn't want them to know I had them, nor did I want them to even see that I had these two parts.

The parts of the car I disassembled were parts of my life that I was handing over to God—my teaching, witnessing, donating time to various organizations, tithing, and things like that. They probably also represented cussing, cocaine, pot, cigarettes, and items like that I was giving to God. The two things I did not want to give were two items I have always had a struggle with. They are the two parts I have battled with for many years and have tried to hold onto, knowing I should have given them up long ago. Let's say they were the two vices I held onto long after giving my life to God—well, most of my life. One of those two things was going to sports pubs every weekend and drinking while watching football and the second was betting on the games. I had a very hard time giving those two things to the Lord.

Another short dream about golfing, but before I share this one, you need to know that I do not play golf, so go figure. There was a golf outing, and I asked the director of this outing if they needed any help or volunteers to do various duties. I was willing to do anything where there may have been a need. I was volunteering for service. As I was asking this man if he needed my help, I was walking up a set of stairs leading away from him at the same time. The stairs were outdoors and led to a rooftop patio. I was asking him if they needed my help while at the same time walking away from the people to whom I was speaking.

When I woke up, this is what came to me. We had just moved from Virginia to California. I didn't know for sure if I was ready to go back into teaching God's Word at our new church. I had been asked several times, and in fact, one of the pastors at one of the two churches we were attending even wrote a letter to me asking me to teach. Teaching, to me, is a major commitment and one that takes a lot of preparation time. Teaching is sort of like adopting a pet or being a foster parent. It's not necessarily a commitment for life, but it is a long enough commitment that you can count on hours of faithful service. I believe in my dream I was asking my new pastor if he needed my help teaching students the Word of God, yet I was walking away from him because I wasn't settled enough into our new home and city to make such a time commitment. But since I've been teaching for so many years and my life has been dedicated to studying the Word of God, in my dream I felt guilty that I was not ready to commit. The current situation in my life corresponded to my dream.

After years of belonging to a Southern Baptist Church in Virginia Beach, Virginia, we wanted to try both a Southern Baptist church as well as a really great church called Cornerstone. Pastor Ron Armstrong has built this church into a great worship center, and for the first time, we considered leaving our Southern Baptist roots.

This is one reason why we have too many different kinds of churches. It boils down to different doctrinal beliefs. Most of today's nondenominational churches believe one can lose one's salvation. The Baptists believe that is not true. Once you're saved, you will always stay that way. Then again, if you say, "I believe in Jesus" yet do nothing about it but say those words once, were they really sincere? It's a close call, but one thing is true: After Jesus went up to heaven, there was one church and one church only. It was called "the way." That's what my license plate says too. There is only one way. I pray that someday some of these churches will merge again into the way.

Here's another short but good dream. A big rig truck was on a snowy street pushing snow up against the cars that were parked. The cars were being covered by the snow as this truck kept barreling down the street and trapping each car. Very few cars had the ability to get out. They were stuck, and only a few strong, persistent cars managed to escape the trap of the snow.

The truck was the Devil, and the snow was the world, with its indulgences, sexual immoralities, and various things the world has to offer. All the temptations, greed, and whatever else that will trap you were represented by the snow. Some of the cars made no effort to get out of the snow and some made major efforts to do so. Many, though, were attempting to escape the grasp of the Devil. Few could get out. There were even people in my dream making an attempt to get out and then giving up. Others I saw kept fighting, yet it seemed too late; the snow had them trapped forever.

Ready? Here's another: There was a war going on or some kind of massive battle. People were looking for weapons everywhere, arming themselves for battle. I, too, was running around preparing to fight in this war. But when I looked at the person next to me, I noticed he was different. He didn't seem human! My conclusion in my dream was that he was a spirit from God. There were masses of men and women eagerly searching high and low throughout the city for guns and other weapons. All the people were frantic and seemed to be very disorganized. Everyone appeared to be determined to find a weapon instead of a hiding place. The spirit who accompanied me and I picked up two forks for weapons. The forks were not made for eating, it appeared, but forks to feed people God's Word.

The forks were the tools needed to eat from the Word of God, or the Bible. It later seemed apparent that those were the weapons that were needed to win that war. The spirit and I were not seeking to destroy but to feed the people the Word of God. The dream was short and to the point, not too much to comprehend.

The next dream was by far the wildest and scariest I had ever encountered in all of my life. Now it wasn't that I was afraid; it was the context of the dream that made it spooky.

While writing this book, I am copying from all my messy and sloppy notes from my many diaries. When you awaken in the middle of the night, you tend to write fast, get it down, and get back to sleep! Your eyes aren't too focused, and it's usually pretty late, so things sometimes get just a little disorganized, especially if you're looking at notes written years ago. I am going to do something a little different for this dream because it's a doozy. When I write down my dreams, I sometimes write only the highlights of them, somewhat like if you write down brief memoirs of a vacation. As you later review the notes of your vacation, you would naturally flash back on even the smallest details because your notes would probably recall only main events during the vacation. That is how I am writing most of this book, from notes and old diaries. This next dream was so intense that I wrote it out almost like a story. Here it is:

Tonight was by far the strangest, most real, and most bizarre dream I have ever experienced. I actually felt like I had crossed over to the third heaven or another dimension. Everything was so real!

A male stranger had approached me and taken me away in this vehicle. I seemed to have been removed from my home physically tonight and was not observing the dream from within my spirit as I normally do. This vehicle appeared to take the shape of an automobile, yet it was more like a machine than a car. The man started to talk to me and led me to believe that I was going to be moving on. Immediately, my first reaction was for my wife, Shar. I had missed her only two seconds after the man told me I would not be returning to her.

I don't know understand why this dream was delivered to me in the way it was, because I have never experienced anything like this before or since. In the past, I had always been aware that I was dreaming. My conscious mind was always partly aware that no matter what happened or where I was in my dream, I was in my bed and asleep.

I wasn't sure if I was ever coming back. I didn't know what had happened to me, but this experience was very different than all the rest. It was real, and I was there! I believed, even though maybe for only a short time, that I might have died in my sleep.

The man who accosted me from my home began to explain to me that this was a metamorphosis that must occur to "go to the other side." He then began to talk and said, "Be patient; these things have to be." Then strange things began to happen all around me, and I became very frightened. There were baby kittens popping up on both sides of the vehicle I was in. Then, as we continued, the kittens became cats and grew larger and aged. In the background, I could hear this soft, peaceful music playing. It was very soothing, yet I was still very afraid. At this point, I started thinking about Shar again and missed her a lot. I had this feeling go through me that something was not right and we were not to be separated in this way. I really missed my wife! I missed Christina, Kelly, and Nicholas too but not in the same way. My spouse was the other part of me, and I felt very much like I was missing *that* part of me. I was aware, or I thought I was aware, that I would never see any of them again.

Then the man spoke to me again and said, "We are going to see your mother." My mother died in 1976 and was a great Christian woman. She was only forty-one years old, so naturally, that was all I needed to hear. I was ready to proceed with him no matter what! It had been more than twenty years since my mother had passed away, and I would have trusted anyone and done anything to be with her and see her again.

Suddenly something struck me and came to the forefront of my mind. Was I really, truly dead! Since I was so used to being aware when I dreamt, I knew this was different. I wasn't aware I was there. This experience was eerie yet at the same time interesting. All these weird things were surrounding me as we sped through this wormhole or light tunnel.

Suddenly, a bright light was shining within this tunnel, and I could hardly stand the glare. I recalled that everything I experienced in the tunnel was so, so beautiful. Yet after I woke, I could not for the life of me remember anything but those cats. I know this for sure: I was very anxious and excited to see my mom.

Then the man spoke to me again, and it seemed like it was such a long time between his verbalizing with me. He slowly turned his head toward me and said, "You will be permitted to go back now and then and visit those you left behind, but they will never be able to see you or know you are there. These times will be designated and appropriated to you as to when and how long you may go. You must go back through the tunnel and visit, but you must always return when you are told." I then proceeded to ask him many questions. I don't remember most of them; I only remember that I kept asking him about many things.

After a very long ride (about two hours in my mind), we came upon this city. We stopped in front of this extremely large mansion. I mean to tell you, this thing was huge. It looked as big as a shopping mall. Then these very nice and attractive ladies came out to greet me. They all looked as if they were in their thirties or forties, but they were very beautiful. They took my hand and led me into a large home, and we came upon a grand staircase. The bottom of the stairwell was very wide, and as one would go up the stairs, it would split off into two directions. Two of the women who brought me into the home suddenly started up the staircase. As they began their ascent, they continued to speak to me. They told me they were going upstairs to get my mother.

A few minutes had passed, and I could see the two women again as they appeared at the top of the staircase and started their descent. I was very anxious. The new woman they were coming down with was wearing a shawl, and I could not see her face. I sort of saw this smile as she looked my way, and again I got very excited. As they got closer and I was able to see the face beginning to form, I knew that it was *not* my mother. Then the two ladies who went up to get her with such looks of peace upon their faces were now coming *down* the stairs with a terrible look of evil. Their faces of beauty had now turned to rotten looks of evil; they looked like death itself.

"That is not my mother," I blurted out with anger. At this time, and in an instant, the peaceful "realness" of this place suddenly left me, and I became immediately aware that it *must* be a dream. "This dream can't be from God because He would never have lied to me!"

The women then started to lunge at me, and I said to them in an angry and determined voice, "I'm going back." The man who brought me to this place then came forward, looked deep into my eyes, and said, "I told you, you can't go back. You can only visit." I looked sternly at him and said, "Oh yeah, watch this!" In an instant, I was shaking my head violently back and forth, with utter determination, and within a second, I was awake and home in bed … of course.

The only true note I made about this dream, I have to say, is a sad one. I was really unable to interpret it. Hardly anything at all came into my mind as I awoke, yet I remembered most of what happened. Here it was, one of the best "real" dreams I had ever experienced, and it wasn't working out for me. I knew one thing for sure was that because the woman wasn't my mother and the ladies turned from nice to evil. For the first time ever, I knew something else could influence my dreams. Could the Devil also talk to me (us) in my (our) dreams? I had to wonder if maybe someone or something could also influence my dreams. This was one of only a few dreams I have ever experienced where I had to question who else could come into my head at night. Without any hesitation, I can say that my Lord would never have caused a dream to come upon me whereby He would have deceived me. So what had just happened?

I think now at this juncture we must pause and pray as to how to recognize a dream from God. The first and foremost thought should be, is this dream against any Scripture? God would never give us a message contrary to His Word. Could the dream just be nonsense or a type of "day at the beach with Nicholas" but in a different style? Whatever the case, the most challenging of all now is this: How does one know if one's dream is from God?

I believe the way to analyze this is to look at Scripture. Did God ever cause anyone to wake up in fear? None of the stories or Scriptures led me to believe this. Did God ever deceive anyone? The answer is no, once again. Would God lead any of us to do something contrary to His Word, our safety, or the safety of our families? The answer to all these, of course, is no! God is a good God; a loving God and a kind God. He wants only the best things in our life, so I believe that when you wake up, He will, *once again*, let you know if it was He that just spoke to you.

Before going to bed that next night and being very angry at the night before, I lay in bed and addressed Lucifer in a verbal voice, saying, "Okay, sucker, you wanna piece of me? Let's go for round two." I was ready to bite off his ear. I was still very irritated from the last dream, especially for messing with my mother. I think we all agree on this: We don't like anyone messing with our mothers! Agreed? Of course, I was speaking to the Devil himself because somehow it had to have been him involved in that dream, so now I needed to find out, "Can Satan enter and influence my dreams too?" If that was the case, I then had a new complication in my discoveries: who, tonight, is influencing my dreams?

I was re-armed, psyched up, and ready to go. I prayed about this night, and I prayed hard. If I was challenging someone who's been around for thousands of years, I knew already that I was the weaker party. Not without Jesus and His blood could I have gone into this type of battle. I was challenging Satan to come at me with all he had because if he was out there, I had to find out about it. If I was going to take on this great challenge of teaching others, I had to go to the front lines and face our enemy. I was anxious for this night and ready to do battle, so here we go.

In my dream that night, there was a bully. He was big, strong, and mean. When I looked at him, it was like I knew him, but I didn't. At times, it seemed like he was sort of a friend, like I felt at home or at ease around him, but then at the same time, I felt uncomfortable too. It was like he was a friendly kind of guy but not for me. This bully seemed to be hanging around me constantly, and I observed him following a few hundred paces behind me everywhere I went. Another unusual thing and why I called him a bully at the start was that he was constantly active and fighting people all around him, in one form or another.

This dude would be walking sort of parallel and slightly behind me, and when he would come upon other people, unprovoked, he would start hassling them, punching them, and just being a bully. Then he would find someone else and wrestle with them or another person and he'd go into this hard-core street fight. Some of the people would even be females. Everything this jamoke did was mean. Every time he would get in these scuffles, I would always be watching him from a bit of a distance. He would always look over at me, but he never physically approached me. It was like I was off limits. I was cautious of him, too, but not afraid of him. I knew he couldn't harm me, yet I didn't want to tangle with him either. I liked the safe distance I was keeping. I was aware of his presence but respectful of his potential.

The bully, if you didn't already figure it out, was the Devil. The people he was beating up were all the people of the world, one at a time, maybe. Could they have been only non-Christians? One wouldn't think so because we, too, have him around us, but still, it was only a dream.

In my next dream, I went back in time to a very happy part of my life. I was living in my childhood home back in the good ol' days. I was looking down at a five-year-old version of myself. I was aware that I was dreaming and was indeed enjoying this dream of being back in that time period of my life. I went to the old barber shop on Belden Avenue called Popeye's. I walked into the Lawson's store, where my mother used to send me to buy bread. Bread was ten loaves for a dollar back then. Wow, what a deal! I visited Belden elementary school and even took a walk to see my old high school, Canton McKinley. I then entered a store because I wanted to buy a cross to wear around my neck. The crosses were made of solid gold and very precious. Everyone wanted one, and everyone knew about them and wanted to get one for themselves. For some reason they were free, too! I got one and then attempted to go back and get another. The lady said, "No, young man, only one per person."

I went down the street to several stores trying obtain or even purchase one of these valuable and precious crosses, but nobody would give me one. In every single store I would enter, the clerks seemed to have this awareness that I had already obtained one of the crosses. When I would ask, they would respond by saying, "You already have one; only one per person." I didn't know how they knew, but they did.

The cross represented Jesus and His salvation. Only one per customer is simple enough, isn't it? He died once and for all of us. I could not get a second cross, nor did He need to die a second time for me or you. Everyone had the opportunity to get one *free* cross. Everyone has the opportunity to accept Him once, too.

If we deliberately keep on sinning after we have received the knowledge of the truth, no sacrifice for sins is left; but, only a fearful expectation of judgment and of raging fire that will consume the enemies of God.' Anyone who rejected the laws of Moses died without mercy on the testimony of two or three witnesses. How much more severely do you think a man deserves to be punished who has trampled the Son of God under foot? Who has treated as an unholy thing the blood of the covenant that sanctified him? Who has insulted the Spirit of grace? For we know him who said, "It is mine to avenge; I will repay," and again, the Lord will judge his people. It is a dreadful thing to fall into the hands of the living God.

(Heb. 10:26–31)

The reason my dream portrayed my childhood was itself easy to conclude; my childhood was simple. I was happy, stress free, debt free, and in no need for complications. The times were only good. The message was plain and simple for me to understand when I awoke. He loves me, and He died once for me! There was no need for two crosses, two Saviors, or two sacrifices, again, once and for all!

Could He also have been telling me to think like a child again? "Unless you become as a child, you shall never see the kingdom of heaven." Children are so simple, so beautiful, and so innocent. I know that is how Jesus wants us to understand and accept His gift.

Let's move on. My wife, Shar, was sitting down at a table. In front of her was some sort of food and what appeared to be a loaf of bread. This food was brought before her by these people who served it to us while we were sitting at the table. Although the food was put before her, she wouldn't eat it. She wouldn't even touch it! She kept staring at the food and did nothing. There were people all around her telling her that she had to accept this food and eat it. The people also insisted that she eat it quickly while she had the chance. They kept persisting with a sense of urgency. It was a gift, they would tell her, and it was there for her to eat right now. In fact, they kept repeating over and over, "Grab and eat."

This dream hurt me a little bit. You see, I was saved as a young man, back in the year 1972, in San Diego, California. When I met my precious wife, I was a Christian but not a practicing one. In fact, I was not the type of man my mother and father brought me up to be. At this time in my life, I've shared with you that I was heavily into cocaine, alcohol, heavy gambling, and this kind of stuff. Although I knew God, I was not walking with Him (Rom. 1:21). Shar knew that I was very learned in God's Word and had studied His Word most of my young life, but I was not practicing the life of a good Christian. It was not until the year 1991 that Shar finally accepted Jesus as her personal Savior. God put my walk back into step after my incarceration, hopefully to get my attention.

I was a very poor mentor, teacher, and leader for my wife our first seven years of marriage. Her dream boiled down to this: The food (to me) was the Bread of Life. Eating it was the accepting and partaking of Christ's body. The people were the people of the church, the body, even maybe His angels. It was my poor example to my wife that made this dream so hurtful to me. *Please* don't make that mistake in your life. If God has called you as a young person to know Him, don't take chances and drift away from your calling—especially to drugs.

Okay, here comes a wild dream: I went into a room or building where it was raining indoors. There was a huge tank of fish in the middle of the room. The fish tank was about the size of a two-car garage. There was yet another room adjacent to the first. It was a cocktail lounge but all disassembled. A lady who was standing there looked at me and said, "You can no longer go into that room. It has been cut off and taken away from you. You must stay in this room." I looked deeply into this second room, the one with the bar, and it was very familiar to me, but I stayed where the lady told me to stay, in the room with the rain and the fish.

This, my friends, is the perfect example of a good and typical dream. The dream is simple and in parable form. Without proper training and education, one would wake up and just say, "Goofy dream," but with proper explanation, I can see God was talking to me in this dream, as well as many others.

The room I was no longer allowed in was, of course, a bar. It represented my years in the bar scene, owning bars and nightclubs and things like that. The room with the fish represented thousands of people who were Christians, especially those in my current church (at that time East Clairemont Southern Baptist). The rain represented the blessings God was giving to us, or maybe it even could have represented some sort of a shelter or baptism. I didn't really know if the rain represented blessings, or comfort, or was the rain even the Holy Spirit? But it was the room in which I was actually allowed to enter and encouraged to stay. The room being dismantled, then, was my old life being slowly removed. This again was a great dream to study.

I liked this next dream a lot! An elderly man took me to a place where there were three pools of water. I could perfectly see that they were not swimming pools but some other type of clear freshwater springs. The man I was with told me to enter the pool with him, so I did. As we were wading into the water, snakes appeared in the water all around me. The man looked into my eyes and said, "Do not be afraid of the snakes. As long as you are with me, they will not harm you." We entered the second pool. Other snakes began to circle me once again but fewer snakes. I felt them all around, but since they did not bother me or attack me in the first pool, I was less afraid. I walked through the water with better faith. Then we headed for the last pool. This time there were so few snakes that I felt in control of them, and my fears were even less than the other two, of course.

I believe that the man was Jesus. Now when I say Jesus, one must understand the man might or might not have been Jesus. I'm not here to tell you what Jesus now looks like. This is a book about dreams, and since I awoke thinking that the man was Jesus, then to me he was Jesus. It was like the bus driver I shared with you earlier in the book. That, if you remember, was my first dream that launched me into these years of study. Well the bus driver looked at me too. I saw his face in my dream, and He represented the Godhead. But at no time do I want anybody out there thinking I'm seeing God. My teaching here is that these things are my dreams. They are parables and manifestations that represent Jesus or God.

I believe the pools had to do with different degrees, plateaus, or steps in my Christian walk. It represented a sort of strength-building knowledge of Him, my Savior, and the confidence I would later have in my Christian walk. Each step (pool) made me stronger in Him. I was less fearful of life's doubts and of course Satan's hold on my hesitation to author this book. As I grew in my own strength and courage, I still recognized the snakes within the water, but I was a stronger man each time I would change pools. God was with me every step of the way.

Okay, here is another dream, but first a preface. There was a time in my life where my businesses were not doing well. I was in a slump. The businesses were either in a slump or *something in my life* just wasn't clicking. I was walking close to God, so I just couldn't figure out why I had come to this dry spell. The finances in our lives had me a little concerned, and I prayed to the Lord asking Him to reveal to me why we were going through this time of famine (so to speak). After those prayers, I had this dream. Oh yeah, we're going to be discussing how to ask God for answers to *your* prayers in your dreams in chapter 7.

I was going to the bank with my business deposits each and every day. As I would enter the bank, the guard would stop me from going into the bank. I would tell the guard that I needed to come in and make a deposit. There were other times when I went, again, into the bank to make a withdrawal, but every time I would go into the bank, this man would stop me in my tracks and would not allow me to enter. When I came in, I would be standing at a counter or teller window of some sort. I would not be allowed inside the heart of the bank itself. As I stood at this teller's window, I would notice other people coming into and leaving the bank freely. It seemed to me like everyone in the world but me was allowed all the way into the bank.

When I awoke that morning, I didn't have much to analyze. For some reason, God was teaching me a lesson in regard to money. I knew that for sure! He wanted me to experience a time of testing. I felt like I was able to feed my family but not do too well other than that. That is why I was able to walk into the bank but only to the doorway. I was being permitted to make a living but not a strong one. I held firm that God would, naturally, *always* love me and this, too, would someday pass … whenever He was ready for it to pass. I had to keep studying and looking for answers. I woke knowing the Lord had a purpose for this time in our lives. During this hard time, I stayed in prayer and faithful to Him, for He has always been faithful to me.

During this period of my life, which lasted about three months, I had another dream in that same format.

I was out doing some shopping for our household. I guess I was at a grocery store. The man at the store was selling beans for a dollar. Yes, a dollar a bean; what a rip-off! Why did I shop there? I would buy several beans, but every time I would make my purchase, I would hand the man a hundred-dollar bill. I would never get any change, though. I kept going back to the store day after day, giving the man a C-note, and getting no change. What a dummy!

Yep, looks like I was headed for a rough time in my life. That's what this dream told me. Because of that, I watched our money carefully during those three months. Maybe that was the lesson in itself, because I never did really figure out why this happened. Was God showing me that I was headed for a rough road ahead and to watch my money? That's what I thought, so I reacted in like manner.

When I pray to God, I always let Him know that I'm constantly looking for his blocks. I call them blocks because I like football so much. I look at God as something like a lineman on an offensive line of a football team. The 'back must always look ahead and be aware of his blockers and then move into the opening left for him. That's how I look for God every day. I look for His blocks. Being a bit of a sports nut, I might as well share another quick metaphor. When I'm praying to God, I sometimes ask Him to simply allow me to get in the game and bunt. In other words, I want to be used by God in *any way* He chooses to use me. In baseball, a bunt is just a man sacrificing to bless the team. I simply ask Him, "Lord, just put me in the game, if even only to bunt."

Going back to the story, I sometimes wondered during these money dreams if maybe I was spending God's money in a different way than He intended. I have thought this through many times, and during this particular time of my life, I was extra careful about the handling of the money He allowed me to have. During this hard period, as always, I stayed in prayer.

Let me share something with you. If you stay in tune with God on a daily basis, you'll find Him working all around you *every* day. The secret is to take notice of everything around you and look for Him in all of it. He uses people as well as a variety of things in and around your life to communicate with you. I've prayed for something a couple of times and found answers in odd places that I really felt were from God.

While driving once, I'd notice a person's bumper sticker and said to myself, "That's *exactly* His answer." Laugh if you want, but as soon as I read those two bumper stickers (on two different occasions), I would myself laugh, and say yes. That was the answer I was trying to find. This has happened to me only twice in my life. Here's what made that bumper sticker my key: As *soon* as I saw them and felt very much that it was the answer to my prayer, I felt complete inside. That was my answer—the feeling of closure on that prayer. So whether it's a friend talking to you, a billboard, a television commercial, a dream, the still, small voice, or the most popular, God's Word, He answers us in many ways. Look for the blocks! Your instincts will probably be right. He places those instincts within us.

Let's get to another dream. In this dream, I went into a restaurant with two of my longtime friends, Marc Bloom and Ralph Vest. We attempted to get into this busy place through the back door. When we arrived at this back door, we noticed we could not fit. The door was too small. So we went around to the front door, entered the restaurant, and ate dinner.

In the tenth chapter of the book of John, Jesus speaks of entering His gate. In order to enter His gate, we need to enter through Him. He says anyone attempting to enter by another means is a thief and a robber. I believe the back door in all my dreams have represented shortcuts. I believe the Lord was showing me, once again, that the only way to Christian maturity is through hard work and dedication. You must devote time in His Word, and there *are no shortcuts*. Once you learn to enter through His gates, the food is plentiful. To give a good testimony, comfort people with their problems, deal with questions about the kingdom, or even just to make a good living one must put in hard work and time dedicated to that work. There are no shortcuts, no back doors.

Let me share one more dream, and then I'm done. Shar and I went somewhere up high, like a mountain or big hill or something like that. We had to climb and climb to get there. Once we arrived, we looked in front of us, and there was the biggest mansion I had ever seen. It was a sight to behold. The beauty of it was spectacular. My pastor, John Swartz, from the church I used to attend in the late '70s,

Bethel Baptist Church of Escondido, California, was passing out leaflets or flyers to everyone coming into this mansion. I guess he was the doorman.

Once inside, I looked to my left and saw these huge rooms. Each room held tens of thousands of people, maybe even millions. Who knows? I remembered that each room was represented by every type of true Christian faith. In one room were the Methodists. They were playing instruments and singing praises to God. In the next room were the Pentecostals. They don't need instruments. They can raise the roof with their praises! The next room was loaded with Baptists. They were petitioning Disneyland (just kidding). The rooms kept continuing down the hall with even more true Christians! Assemblies of God, Seventh-Day Adventists, Lutherans ...

That's it! I woke up, and it was simple for me to see. The big house was heaven, and the rooms were full of different kinds of denominations of true believers of God's Word. The rooms then represented the many kinds of true faith believers who have their place in God's kingdom. One thing that took me a while to figure out was why those rooms were only on one side of the hall. But once I thought long and hard about it, it had to be for those guys at Calvary Chapel. I checked with reservations, and they are holding a huge reunion up there some day. They will need all the room they can get! (Sorry, that was a joke too; I love the Calvary Chapel churches.)

Well, friends, how many more do you want? I can keep giving you my life's stories by sharing my dreams, day after day and week after week, but by now I hope you got the point. I've given you a well-rounded array of how my dreams reflect my daily life. This long chapter was meant for you to see that my dreams are probably no different than yours. This chapter wasn't meant to impress you; in fact, just the opposite.

Remember this: a man's dreams are a reflection of his everyday life. Now it's up to you to start writing your dreams down and asking God to work in your life and of course throughout the night. I'm telling you this with assured confidence, so "for those who have an ear, let them hear": God wants more of you! He wants you to read his book (the Holy Bible) more, pray more often, and worship and recognize Him in your everyday life. I think it might not be possible for you to ask for dreams without having a prior relationship with Him anyway. I don't know for sure, but because I know Him and He knows me, He feeds me many dreams. I have no authority to say this, but it is my opinion that the only way to get to know God at night is to first know Him during the day. Study His Word, spend a half an hour a day in prayer, and sing psalms to Him during your day. Sing while you wash dishes, sing while you fold clothes, sing to yourself at work, whatever you do, sing praises to the Lord.

CHAPTER 6

My God, Why Can't I Sleep?

When you lie down, you will not be afraid; when you lie down, your sleep will be sweet.

(Prov. 3:24)

Have you ever awakened in the middle of the night and found you were unable to fall back to sleep again? Did you then toss and turn, battling intently to try to get your mind to just settle down and relax? After being woken up for what seems like no reason at all, maybe you got up out of bed, grabbed something to drink, or even read a few chapters of a book. Maybe you just stayed right there snug in your bed, hugging your favorite pillow, hoping it would put you back to sleep.

I think we have all had this experience many times in our lives. Allow me to share something you might not realize. Have you ever thought that maybe God is trying to get your attention during these wee, quiet hours of the night? Has it ever crossed your mind that the Creator may want to use this quiet time to talk with you? Or maybe He has *always* used this time to speak *deep* into our hearts. Ya know, maybe He's waking you for a reason.

This is exactly what may be happening, and that's what we're going to discuss in this chapter. Please allow me to make you aware of what may be occurring and how to recognize when God is tapping on your shoulder.

Of course, we sometimes wake up for various other reasons, as well. A noise outside often can wake us in the middle of the night. The children might be crying because they might have had a bad dream. A fever, the flu, a cough, or even a sore throat could wake you. But what you're looking for here is the stirring of God Himself asking for your undivided attention. You see, God, too, will keep you awake to get your attention. I knew before I began this study, I'd just about collapse from exhaustion. I'd be so tired but couldn't sleep. It's important to know when God is knocking on your door, so pay attention.

In a dream, in a vision of the night, when deep sleep falls on men as they slumber in their beds, he may speak in their ears and terrify them with warnings, to turn man from wrongdoings and keep him from pride to preserve his soul from the pit, his life from perishing by the sword.

(Job 33:15–18)

I was living in Virginia Beach, Virginia, back in 1997, when a dear friend, George Faatz, mentioned to me that he was waking in the middle of the night and was not able to go back to sleep. Not many people would instinctively think that if they woke up during the night it would be God doing the waking.

This has always been my belief during this study of dreams. God seems to have wakened me on many nights. Thanks be to the Holy Spirit, I've recognized His signature. So when I wake in the middle of the night, and for reasons not related to body chemistry (gotta go to the bathroom), health problems, or a conscious effort to wake up to log in a dream, I've immediately concentrated entirely and wholly on God.

Train up a child in the way he should go, and when he is old he will not turn from it.

(Prov. 22:6)

Maybe it was all the Bible teachings from my mother when I was young lad. The lessons my mom taught me have lasted a lifetime. I cherish the days my mother read and taught the Bible to me. She would at times come running to me at night as I would cry out to her in the darkest hours. I might have simply been afraid of the night sky or maybe a noise or even a bad dream. Since I was a first child, my mom would always comfort my childish fears and explain to me that "Jesus would lay things on my heart" during those dark hours and to concentrate on Jesus! Wow, what a cool mother I had.

My mom would further explain to me that although the nightmare may have come from the thoughts running through my brain, it was God who *woke me* and was waiting to now converse with me. From that time, even from my youngest memories, I see my mother explaining to me small, still voice and how He was best heard in the stillness of the night.

> **Find rest, O my soul, in God alone; my hope comes from Him.**
>
> (Ps. 62:5)

As I grew a little older and would wake in those wee hours of the night, I began a lifelong nighttime relationship with the Lord. So even as a child, the Lord Jesus Christ was not someone I grew up with only in the daytime hours, nor was He someone I grew in knowledge of only on Sundays. *No,* the Jesus my mother taught me to love, I recognized in the day *and* in the darkest hours of the night. I found this relationship with Him to be the most valuable of all. Dark, quiet, and alone … and surely not afraid. Now wouldn't you like to know Him like that as well?

> **Does He not see my ways and count my every step.**
>
> (Job 31:4)

So when my friend George mentioned this sleeping problem to me, he seemed to be a little stunned that I took it in sort of lightly and looked no further than what I have explained here. Ya know, I think it was because of the instruction I received as a child to search in my heart for God at night.

When *your* evening comes and when *you* lay down in your bed for the night with all of life's problems running through your head, don't look at this time as God talking to you; that's not God! In fact, He commands you not to worry (Phil. 4:5). That doesn't mean not to pray. By all means, give God your cares and concerns, and allow Him to help you *get* to sleep.

I won't ever believe our Lord would be *keeping us awake* so we can worry about tomorrow. As mortals, we tend to review the current day's bummers, and of course, our next day's problems too. At the time of day where we are supposed to be settling in and kicking back, relaxed, many of us are worrying about the money needed to be made, the bills piling up, our spouses, our children, and a whole mess of other things. So here it is, the time of day when our body insists that we rest up and prepare for the next day of life, but instead … we lay there and worry.

There are many Scriptures that instruct us not to worry. Jesus spoke of not worrying when He was sharing with us how much the Father cared for us and how He feeds the birds.

> *Therefore I tell you, do not worry about your life, what you will eat or drink; or about your body, what you will wear. Is not life more important than food.*
>
> (Matt. 6:25)

So again, the problems in our lives are not the theme of our discussion in this chapter. What I am about to share with you is a different type of insomnia. In fact, let's not call it insomnia. It's more of an awakening or God tapping on your brain, saying, "Wake up, I am talking to you." It's this special conversation in the middle of the night, that we're talking about here.

I want to explain to you what occurs when you suddenly, without apparent reason, find yourself with your eyes wide open, unsure as to why on earth you've suddenly awakened—and more than that, why you can't fall back to sleep.

You're not sick with the flu, *and* you didn't hear anything go "bump in the night"; you've simply opened your eyes and now are wondering why.

The first thing to be aware of is this how to *always* be aware of God and how He interacts in our lives both in the day and in the night. Many people are only accustomed to worshiping or communicating with God in just a few areas of their lives. We naturally know prayer is one of these areas in which we speak to God and listen for Him to answer us. We've all heard it said that God answers usually one of three ways: yes, no ... or wait.

When we devote time to reading our Bibles, we are coming to God and attempting (hoping) to clear our minds and spend quality time with the Him as well. At least that's what we intended to do. We also come to God with songs and psalms. We worship Him, and we communicate as we praise Him in that special style of worship and adoration. I've got to admit, for the daytime fellow Christians, those are the main sources of communication with our Lord. But He also speaks to us in *so* many other ways that, unless you are aware of these ways, you're not getting the total fulfillment our Lord had planned for you when He adopted you into His family!

> ***My eyes stay open through the watches of the night, that
> I may meditate on your promises.***
>
> (Ps. 118:148)

I want you to understand something special here! I want you to be constantly aware of how God is *with you* in *all* things you do. Sometimes God uses other people and circumstances in an attempt to try and communicate with you. I use the word *try* because there are times when He's talking to you and some of you are not even aware of how many ways the Holy Spirit can actually speak to you. The first thing we have to do is make you aware of the many different ways the Holy Spirit works. Therefore, part of this chapter's study is to expand on three typical ways of listening for God in ways outside of your daily prayers, songs, and reading of His Word.

Halt!

Before we go any further, I need to clear a path and make something perfectly clear: I am in *no way* replacing prayer, reading of God's word, or singing praises to the Lord! Not a chance! We are simply studying, expanding, and exploring other ways of acknowledging *Him* and how He sends the Comforter to speak to us.

The first way is He sometimes uses people *around you* to communicate to you. Be aware that when you are in prayer about something, God often uses other things like friends, Christian radio programs (CSN is my favorite—Calvary Satellite Network), and sometimes even something as simple as a billboard. Each of these might have the answer to that prayer.

You see, God can use other people to bring an answer to your prayers. So stop, think, and listen. The words just spoken out of your neighbor's mouth just might have been the answer you were searching for in regard to your prayer. God doesn't have a rule that says all His responses have to come from the Bible, per se. For instance, if you have been praying for a particular job and that job comes through, one might conclude that God has answered your prayer in a direct way. He didn't necessarily answer that prayer through His Word, meaning the Bible. You prayed for the job, and He granted it to you.

Praise God! There was your answer to prayer. It didn't come from the Bible or from hearing His voice; it just came.

Let's also say you were praying about your broken-down automobile. You prayed and asked God that it would not be too expensive to fix. Part of that prayer was that the repair shop would be honest and fair about the work they would perform. In fact, you may have already had the worst assumptions that maybe you blew your engine. Only later you find out it was only a blown freeze plug. Was that an answer to prayer? *You better believe it!* To a believer, this *was* answered prayer. To an unbeliever, it is simply good luck.

I mentioned in an earlier chapter about an answered prayer that came to me through a bumper sticker. In fact, this has happened to me twice in my life. God, in His infinite wisdom, placed me behind a car whose message to me was the answer to my prayer. *Your* bumper sticker answered *my* prayer!

God uses all kinds of people in our lives, as well as many other avenues, to answer our prayers, but of course studying His Word and keeping ourselves in direct prayer will always be the Lord's main avenue of communication with us, His people.

The secret here is to keep in tune with Him. Look for Him in all situations, in all hours of the day, and through everything you do in your life; simply put, *look for God.*

I think that's what Paul meant when he said, "I pray continually." I don't think Paul prayed all the day long, per se, but I do think he kept a conscious awareness of maintaining a portion of his thoughts constantly in prayer. Don't laugh at me, but I want to share something with you that I shared with my Bible study group. I lead a group of wonderful people called CBMC (Christian Business Men's Committee), but our chapter has females as well. You'll find CBMC in many cities in the United States and in fact throughout the world.

Anyway, have you ever minimized something at the bottom of your computer? In other words, the program is still running (in the background), but you're now working on something else. At the bottom of your screen that other thing is simply there, running. That's what I think Paul meant when he said, "Pray continually." In a part of my brain, God is always running, never turning Him off, never X-ing Him out. Yes, I surely do other things ... but God is running in the background, *if not in the foreground,* at all times.

> **His eyes are always on the ways of men; He sees their every step.**
>
> (Job 34:21)

Remember, keep your ears listening and your eyes watching. Look for Him and look for His communication (clues) all around you, every day, all of the time. Keep God a part of your life all hours of the day and *all* hours of the night. Now let's look at God speaking to you at night.

> **When you are in your beds, search your hearts and be silent.**
>
> (Ps. 4:4b)

When I wake up in the middle of the night and listen to that quietness of the evening, my first thoughts are about the Lord. I was raised as a child to think this way, and the older I get, the greater this relationship has grown. It is so quiet and still at this time of night, and my wife is usually fast asleep. Oh, and by the way, Shar doesn't snore! (Uhh-ummm.) At this hour, the phone doesn't ring, and my three parrots, Beauty, Popcorn, and Chewy, are (finally) quiet as mice. It seems that it's this stillness of the night that God looks for this grand opportunity where He has me *and* my thoughts ... *and* alone. So the next time *you* are awakened in the middle of the night by something and you find yourself not falling directly back to sleep, stop and ponder, *What is it He wants me to think about?*

Let me remind you. Now is *not* the time to think about how your car is running. It is also the *worst* time to think about buying a new television set or who you might ask out on a date next week or how you're going to scrape up the money to pay the rent—or any and *all* those other earthly, material types of thoughts. I say it's the worst time because you are wasting the most precious opportunity God has to communicate with you. It is the peace and quietness of His nights that *He is looking for you.*

I love those that love me and those that seek me, find me.

(Prov. 8:17)

So get your thoughts off (or out) of the earth and into heaven. Please take notice that Jesus stayed in unbroken prayer and fellowship with His Father! And in fact, Jesus found it necessary to be in quiet solitude with His Father as well. I think we Christians call this "quietude." In your Bible, take note of the times that Jesus went alone to pray to the Father (Mark 1:35; Matt. 14:23; Luke 6:9, 12, 18, 29; 22:41). This alone time is harder for us today because of the hustle and bustle of our lives. It is at this time there are no telephones, cell phones, texts, knocks on the doors, or kids playing all around you, and the dog isn't barking. It is this most valuable quiet time, at night, where God is now calling *you* and saying, "Hey, we're finally alone."

Peace, be still, and know that I am God.

(Ps. 47:10)

Psalm 47:10 is one of my all-time favorite verses, so be still and think on God and He will put into your mind thoughts far beyond earthly problems and worries. Today's problems and other thoughts can all wait. They will all be there in the morning, so don't think about them—*not* at this time; this is His time. Remember that. Concentrate on that, and you will develop the warmest and most intimate relationship with the Lord.

During the night, God will deliver to you that small, still voice we all search for and have heard about. And why? *Because He has you all to Himself!* It's just you and God—the King of the universe ... and *hey*, think about this: He wants to talk to you. The phone won't ring. Your husband, wife, children, parents, friends, neighbors, and even the bill collectors can't disturb you during this private time in the middle of the night.

God has called on you, so answer Him. He wants to talk to you, only you, so stop and listen. Meditate on Him and what He is trying to communicate with you. Trust me on this: your life will *never* be the same.

You know, folks, I have always considered it an honor and a privilege when He wakes me and calls me into His presence. In fact, when I wake in the middle of the night—let's say, once every two weeks—I picture myself right in front of His throne. As soon as my eyes open and I see the hour on the clock, the first words out of my mouth are, "Yes, Lord," and *I wait. In silence ... I wait.*

Ya know, here's something else I've *never* shared, ever, with anybody. Right now as I'm editing this book, I'm adding this. God always seems to wake me at 3:33 a.m. sharp. *Bam*, just like that; what cool numbers! I've got goose bumps even right now! I can't believe how often I'll wake, look at my digital clock, and it'll say 3:33 a.m.

There were years when I'd wake in the middle of the night and just lay there, a bump on a log. You see, I'm beyond that now, so I've learned that the moment I wake, it's Him waking me. Now I don't ponder; I get right to His business.

Have you ever had the thought of how privileged Abraham or Moses were to know God? Have you ever thought how cool it would have been to be Paul, or how 'bout Isaiah, or even Jacob? Just think— wouldn't it have been to have known God in that capacity? If you answered yes, then wake up; we're no different than they were. I believe 100 percent that I *do* have that same relationship they did. The difference is, I listened for God and implemented that relationship. It's there for me. In fact, it's there for you too, just live the life; walk the walk and talk the talk.

> **Wait for the Lord; be strong and take heart and wait for the Lord.**
>
> (Ps. 27:14)

So what do I concentrate on, you ask? How do I know when He's talking to me? What do I talk about with Him? Now hear this: you only have one job to do; He'll provide the conversation. Here is your job, and this is all you have to do: *Concentrate on not allowing your mind to wander.* That's it! And this is *very* important: *stay focused on God*. If you want God to speak to you, then you must concentrate and not allow your brain to think about earthly things, for you are worshiping in spirit.

Your duty is simple. Keep the train on the track, and allow your mind to stay open for business. Concentrate only on Him, and then allow the Conductor of life, the Holy Spirit, to run that train, which, of course, is your brain (or your thoughts). He will come to you, and you will enjoy some of the best worship time you have ever experienced.

One of my favorite books is Tommy Tenney's *God Chasers*. Tommy talks about being such a child of God. It's like going up to your daddy, as a child, and tugging at his pants leg. The Father is going to look down at your tugging, smile, and say, "Now that's the kind of child I want with me—the one who chases after Me." Remember, "Seek and ye shall find." His promises *aren't* shallow

Have you ever been to a Greg Laurie Harvest Crusade or another type of revival, like a Billy or Franklin Graham Crusade? Or have you ever attended a very special church service where you pastor has just been anointed by the Holy Spirit and you just *know* this day is special? Have you ever heard a message over the radio or on TV and that message just touched your heart more than usual? This is the kind of experience God will give to you in the middle of the night. Why? Because it's special, quiet, and very personal.

The Father rarely has you like this. You can be sure He's going to use this time for a wonderful period of growth and closeness. Look forward to it! Count on it! Have faith in Him. He will provide. Just don't forget your job. Seek Him, concentrate only on Him, and be patient. Don't be hurrying God to come do this in a night or two either. That would be like the guy who never prays but then in the hospital he gets down on his knees promising God he'll solve the hunger problems of the world if God just does this or that for him. God wants to see change. He wants to see commitment. He wants to be closer to you!

> *I will instruct you and teach you in the way you should go; I will counsel you and watch over you.*
>
> (Ps. 32:8)

What if I don't feel anything or I can't keep focused? In that case, then just start to pray. Generally when I pray, I pray aloud. Rarely do I pray in the quietness of my head, in silence. I was always raised as a child to pray aloud. I'm not loud with my prayers, of course. But I do express my prayers in a quiet, verbal voice. Now when I pray at night, I pray even more quietly. The night is silent, so I keep within the mood of that silence. Plus, Shar is sleeping.

So, if I'm in my bed in the middle of the night, my first thought is to keep my mind quiet, open, and focused. If my mind wanders (and it does; I am human), I simply start to pray and keep the prayer focused. He will then come to me, and our conversations will begin. But I try hard not to allow myself to think about tomorrow's workday or anything other than the fact that God has just woken me, so I'd better concentrate on Him. Sometimes I might sing a praise song quietly or even in my head.

Okay, one of two things now happens. First, I (or you) will fall back to sleep, and there's nothing wrong with that because *He has allowed me to.* Or I will stay awake and wait on Him. Now, by falling back to sleep, you must understand, I haven't gone away from His will. I haven't rejected Him, and I haven't made Him mad at me. He has the ability to keep me awake or to put me to sleep. The Holy Spirit controls my every move, so falling back to sleep must have been the plan. I don't get mad that I fell back to sleep. Now if I pray and do not fall back to sleep, then I am even more convinced that the Holy Spirit and I have got ourselves some real business to attend to! I'm 100 percent sure of this.

So, as best I can, I lay still and concentrate on Him first. If that doesn't work and I find myself drifting, like I explained earlier, I start to pray. I might stop in my prayer and again wait on Him, pray, and then wait some more. The Holy Spirit will deliver the message. He works twenty-four hours a day, and He hears our prayers every day, all the time. You will never fail at this, folks. God wants to talk to you. The Holy Spirit, the Comforter, has things He wants you to think about. Just stay faithful. Faithful in this case means to have faith God will communicate with you. This is the reason I am writing this book. The end is very near, my friends, and it is time to be aware that the Holy Spirit is going to be pouring Himself out to us in these latter days. Do you want to be part of that pouring? I think you do, so here's your 101 class.

I mentioned a little earlier in the chapter that I loved the apostle Paul's words, "Pray without ceasing" (1 Thess. 5:17). You may think this is hard to do, but in one of the books by O. Hallesby called *Prayer*, Mr. Hallesby's son, at the time of writing, a very young man, comes into Mr. Hallesby's study. Knowing not to disturb his father, the boy simply states, "Papa, I will sit still all the time if you will only let me be here with you." Hallesby continues to share how he listened to his son's remarks and then reflected on them, and then related them to God.[2]

May I always be in Thy presence, oh Lord. I have nothing more to say to Thee, but I do love to be in Thy presence. *Wow, did that strike home!* These words, brought on by a little boy, will be something I too will cherish as long as I walk on this earth. Lord, just allow me to be near You, all the time, without ceasing. Even if I've got nothing to say, can I just lay here and think on You. I don't know about you, but I've got tears in my eyes just thinking about that simple kind of love!

Let's move on to the third step we are dealing with in this chapter— an even greater plateau.

You might, at times, find yourself combining this quiet time of prayer and meditation (at night) with a dream that has just occurred that same night. Let's now take a look at this scenario.

It is nighttime, and you just had a wonderful dream! The dream is now over and you wrote it down, and now you lay back down to continue your sleep. Now think about this for a moment! Isn't this about as good as it gets? First of all, you went to bed and fell asleep. Then you had a dream. You then woke up and remembered your dream, and now you've just written it down. Maybe you've hit it *really* big and even received a message and an interpretation of the dream too. Now you're lying there in bed and it's still the *wee* hours of the night. Well, praise the Lord what else can you want? You've got it all—the dream, the interpretation—and now He's waiting on you to be still so He might lay something upon your heart. It might even be that He wants to talk about the dream He just gave you.

---

2   O. Hallesby, *Prayer.*

I think in hockey they call this a hat trick. In baseball, it's a grand slam, and in a Christian's life it's called the Super Bowl of blessings. Enjoy this night.

You see, you might have earlier looked at this type of scene and thought, *Man this dream thing is for the birds. I had this dream and now I can't fall back to sleep. Why did I ever read this book?* Sure, look at it that way if you want, but you can also look at it as the greatest blessing one can ever have.

There's something positive about waking up in the night and not being able to fall back to sleep. Think on Him, and He'll put you back to sleep. Think on things of the world and you'll be up the whole cotton-pickin' night. You'll fall asleep a lot faster if you concentrate on God. I can't tell you why, but it just works that way. He talks to me, and then He puts me back into a great rest. And by meditating on Him during this time, I usually have yet another great dream, even better than the first.

My heart gets deeper and deeper into God the older I get, and my brain gets more attentive to God and His will. Believe this, you guys—this gift of dreams and talking with God at night will just grow and grow in you. Think about this: don't you think God *wants* this from you? Don't you realize that *nothing* pleases God more than Him knowing how much you love Him and that you want to spend more time with Him? Wouldn't you think that God will just love to have you respond to the dream He puts in your head? Therefore, develop the deepest relationship with Him both day and night. Of course He wants that; do you?

> **Come near to God and he will come near to you ...**
>
> (James 4:8)

I believe that James, the half-brother of Jesus, sure knew this well when he wrote down those precious words. James lived them. In fact,

I think that's why he wrote about them. And now I, too, have lived this book, and that's why I am writing about it! God can't really come closer to you until you first choose to allow Him to. And that can't be done until you *first* draw close to Him. Believe it or not, it's *you* who holds the decision to allow Him in or shut Him out.

> **Behold I stand at the door and knock. If anyone hears my voice and opens the door, I will come in ...**
>
> (Rev. 3:20)

Hey, gang, who is doing the knocking here? Jesus—right? 'Cause it's not you. And who opens the door? You do! Have you grasped this yet? He's knocking on *your* door. What door? The door to your heart; so now think this through!

You, then, are opening it up and letting Him in. He's not forcing you to do this; *He's giving you the option.* I can't stand it when I hear someone say God is dead. I haven't really heard this (publicly) since the mid-'60s, but now it's surfacing once again. He wasn't dead then, and He's not dead now. We're the ones who may have been dead. Once we stopped growing and started splitting the body of the church into little pieces, well, that's what the Holy Spirit had to work with. We are called the church body. How strong would your body be if it was broken up into pieces?

Anyway, back to Revelation 3:20. I'm sure Jesus wasn't talking about lying in bed and knocking on the door of your heart, but it doesn't mean He could not have been also referring to that too! Behold, while you are lying in your bed at night, He is standing at the door of your heart and knocking. If you hear Him *and* open the door, He'll come in and talk with you, in the deepest part of your heart and soul, He'll talk to you. So at night when you are laying there in bed, listen for His knock. Oh, He'll knock all right. He promised us He would. All of us? Well, He sure didn't say just for the Jews or for the Gentiles but all of us! I've been listening to Him while putting this book together for many years. And ya know, I'm not in an exclusive club. Look closely at how the Holy Spirit has been stirring things up in the past few decades.

It took a spark to get that fire blowing, and now the spark is lighting again. A long time ago, that spark was represented by the tongues of fire back in the beginning of Acts. It was during that time, and now, that represented a big-time work of the Holy Spirit. I am confident that many are getting a spark here in today's times. The beginning of the end is upon us. Get close to Him now; He's out there knocking. Let Him deeper and deeper into your life. Get the full enjoyment of the Spirit, who gives to us generously!

CHAPTER 7

Ask, See, and Find

This chapter is dedicated to Darren Davis. His tragic
death caused me to finish this chapter, which has
eluded its final stage for more than a year.

*Ask and it will be given to you; seek and you will find;
knock and the door will be opened to you. For everyone
who asks receives; the one who seeks finds; and to the one
who knocks, the door will be opened.*

(Matt. 7:7–8)

Here we are ... this is it, folks—the true study on how to have the
most incredible relationship with God at night! Up to now, I've taught
you how to remember your dreams, how to write down your dreams,
and how God—and only God—will give you the interpretation of
those dreams.

Now we will study the depths of communication with God during
the night. This is the most exciting relationship you can ever imagine.
To be honest, many of you will not get to this level, *but* hundreds of
thousands of you will.

There's nothing like a good story, so let me share with you one of the
first times this worked for me, and then you can decide what you

111

think. My next-door neighbors were going through a terrible time in their lives. They were arguing over everything. Shar and I had brought them to church; both had gone forward and accepted the free gift of salvation. The husband actually got baptized in our swimming pool with many others from my church. The wife was baptized earlier in life.

But now they were arguing again, and geez, this one was a doozy. The husband came over to our house and told us he was going to leave his wife. He had it; he was done, and she seen her last days with him. He didn't bring a suitcase with him, but I saw that look on his face; he wanted to stay with us. I didn't invite him to move in or anything; I just told him things would get better and that we'd be praying for him.

That night I asked God to speak to me—to give me His instructions as to how I should handle my neighbors. I really prayed hard on this, guys. I wanted the Lord to truly instruct me on what I should do with this couple. Here was my dream.

I was walking down a street in the mid-afternoon, just pacing at sort of a slow walk. I remembered the sun was beating down on me, and I was feeling good. I think I was even whistling a little tune. I was looking around at the buildings, the parks, and other things around me when all of a sudden I saw a building down the street with many people on ladders painting the building.

I approached the building and felt it was odd that there were about forty men and women painting it. Not only that, but everybody who was painting was up on a ladder, and the ladders were only about one foot in space from each other. So envision this if you will: we've got like forty people, side by side, up on the top floor of a five-story building, all painting.

Up on the roof was a man pacing back and forth. I could tell right away he was the foreman. His hands were behind his back as he watched each person doing his or her respective job of painting the building. When he reached the end of the row of painters, he swung around and headed back in the other direction. As he walked firmly and with authority, I watched him go back and forth a few times.

For about five minutes I watched all the people when suddenly two of them fell off their ladders and hit the ground. I immediately sprung up to jump to their aid, only to find they weren't really hurt. I had assumed they surely would have at least broken some bones.

That wasn't the case, so I approached the two who had fallen to offer them a lift up when all of a sudden the foreman yelled from the roof, "*Hey … you*! Don't you dare touch those people. Those are my people; they work for me. They have to learn, and the only way they will learn is by falling and starting again, falling and trying again."

I looked up at this guy with a curious look and attitude on my face, like, "Why can't I just offer them a hand up?" My hand was still sort of down by my side, as if to help one of the two back up on their feet, when here comes that voice again. "Hey, I asked you kindly. Now please … don't bother those two; they need to learn. Just please allow them to get up on their own two feet."

Folks, when I woke up, I remembered every single part of that dream. As soon as I woke up, I related that dream to the two people who lived next door. Now was I right? Gosh, I'm never sure if I'm ever really right; I live by faith.

I live each and every day with the knowledge in mind that I've got a close and intimate relationship with the Father. If I approach Him in prayer and ask Him to talk to me in my dreams, then I surely wake up expecting and anticipating hearing from Him. So, yeah, I'm pretty sure that was what the dream was all about.

About ten minutes went by, and my six-year-old grandson, Nicholas, woke up and came outside to the patio where we were having our morning coffee and orange juice. Nick was rubbing his eyes, and he looked over to his YaiYai and me (my wife, Shar, of course, is YaiYai) and said, "Papo, I had this really weird dream last night. We were in this big boat. There were all kinds of people in this boat, and we were moving pretty slow on the water."

He continued, "Then two of the people in the boat fell into the water and you ran over to where they fell in and put your hand down to help them back in the boat. Then the Captain of the boat looked at you from on top of where he was steering the boat, and he said, 'Hey you, yeah you, don't touch those two people. They have to learn, and this is the only way they are going to learn.' You tried to help them, Papo, but the Captain wouldn't let you."

Needless to say, folks, I began to cry. Not only did God give me the dream I was hoping for (an answer), but He also gave a dream to Nicholas, as innocent as a young man can be, to deliver to me that dream, which pretty much was as close to my dream as could be.

After wiping up my tears, I asked, "What happened after that, Nick?" He said, "The rest was really weird too; the people never did come up from the water. They went through the water and came out the other side."

I questioned Nick to find out further what he meant. Nick expressed the rest of the dream with his hands. He showed me how the people fell into the water, sunk down under the water, and came out below, where, as Nick said, "There was air." I asked again, "You mean they didn't come up the same way?" He said, "No, it seems they had to go down into the water to get the fresh air from the other side."

Here we go again; my eyes began to well up with tears as I praised my Lord and God, who is so gracious to give a young, young boy such a dream. Nick could not have explained that dream any better. These people had to go *through* their problems in order to come up the other side of them. I wasn't permitted to help with the two who fell off the ladder, and I wasn't able to help the two who fell off the boat. In both cases God was telling me, "Hey, I got this covered" Funny!

You might say that was one of the first dreams followed by many years of talking to God and getting answers from Him while I sleep. And remember, just like all the other dreams and stuff we talked about in earlier chapters, sometimes there are no answers. Or ya know what? Maybe sometimes I just might have messed up and not remembered them.

But even during this what I call the request for dreams part of dreaming, sometimes God just doesn't have to answer me, or maybe it's just something He just chooses not to address. If that weren't so, I'd be asking every night for Him to just, "Speak to me, dear God." For those of you who know God, we often say God has three answers: yes, no, or not now.

We adult humans are kind of like children in many ways. Wouldn't we want our fathers to come and sit next to our beds and talk with us as we slumber into the night? I believe so!

God is there every day to love you, and don't you forget that. Now, do you think—and seriously, answer this truthfully—do you think He wants to give me and me *only* these dreams? Do you think God wants only me to answer only my dreams, like I'm somebody extra special? *Not a chance!* If there's one thing I know about my (oops, our) Lord, it is that He loves each of us—not me more than you and not you more than me.

So that means for you to learn how to fly a plane, you need to take lessons. You need to practice, and you need to fall off your ladder and get back up and try again. Don't be impatient with God; He's truly not going to be impatient with you.

God's time stands still forever. Today is like yesterday to God. He's got no calendar up there in heaven, and He's not counting the days you've messed up and not prayed or asked Him for a dream or asked Him for some help. He's there to love you, to teach you and to watch *you* grow.

Now please listen, because this is important. Don't skip the lessons taught in the earlier chapters on how to interpret your dreams, how to remember your dreams, etc., because you need to get those basics down before asking God for specific dreams.

I say this from many years of experience. You've just *have* to put the order of things right here. First just pray before bedtime and acknowledge to God that you've just read the manual on dreams. Then let Him know this is what you want in your life: *to know Him more.* In your prayers tonight, share with Him that this book you just read has excited you and that *you* want some of this relationship with Him too. Ask *Him* to teach you. This book is only a guide to get you started. *Hey,* this is His world, His communication—you might say His game. I'm only a player … okay, maybe a coach?

God loves when we grow, ya know. I mean, c'mon, folks; do you have children? Isn't it the coolest thing to see your young children learn something new? The first time they walk, talk, go to school, play an instrument, or score their first points playing a sport, get their first job, or bring home their first paycheck is awesome. We never stop wanting to watch our children grow and become more adult and mature.

You think we humans are exclusive with that sort of excitement? Fah-get about it! Our Father gets more excited than we do. He wants you to lead others to know Him. He craves for you to invite someone to join you at church. God waits for you to join a Bible study or have one at *your* home. Your growth is what being born again is all about. You've been born again into the family of Jesus Christ—so grow!

Now, to dream and to understand your dreams, well let's call that elementary school. This next level moves us out of elementary school and on to high school and maybe even college. Once you've graduated from this elementary-type level of dreams, now begin to practice asking Him to communicate with you.

He wants this! Hey, are you getting this? *He wants it.* He wants you to know He's there. He wants you to come to Him with your problems and questions. He wants to sit at the end of your bed and talk with you while you are dreaming. He wants you to read His Word, go to church, pray, study, pray, and study some more. And believe this: He doesn't just want dreamers.

You can't go to college without first going through the basic courses of life, *even* if that means your Christian life.

This is a funny thing I often think about. To God there is no time; *time stands still.* So if you die one day without *ever* talking (or praying) to God, when you get before the judgment seat in heaven, I believe He will say to you, "I was there every day with you; not a moment of your life was I not right beside you. You never said good morning to me; you never said thank you, and you never asked me for help when I was actually just a prayer away from you. In fact, you never even said hello. I waited for you; I hoped you would come to me, but you didn't."

But I have to pause here to say this *one more time* because it's really important. Nothing but nothing takes the place of God's Word, our Bible. There will be no dream that God gives you that will be contrary to His Word. For example, God loves marriage, so don't wake one day and try to convince me that God told you it's time for a new wife. Gosh I make myself laugh!

Our precious heavenly Father is the same yesterday, today, and forever. Remember the words of Pastor Greg Laurie, "If it's new, it's not true, and if it's true, it's not new." That's such a great measuring rod.

I've had some terrible nightmares from some of my prayer requests too. In fact, some are too tragic to even put into this book. I've prayed about people's salvation; I've prayed about heaven and yes, even hell. Some of the places my dreams have taken me could cause Hollywood to make the most terrible scary movies. But you know what? I never was scared while having those dreams. They were the most gruesome, monstrous images, but God kept me comforted.

Remember in the first few pages of this book I shared with you that toward the end of days our Bible says, (my paraphrase) we shall dream dreams and have visions. Well don't forget what I'm about to say here; I've taken more than twenty years studying and preparing this book.

This chapter, though it's not the last chapter of this book, it was (or is) actually the last chapter I wrote. I just had the hardest time completing this chapter.

Lately there hasn't been anywhere I go that I don't find people talking about dreams. I hear it more now than ever. I explained to you in an earlier chapter that people came up to me with their dreams, *not knowing* I was writing about dreams. Well, that was child's play compared to what I hear at church, at the mall, in a restaurant, or on the beach *today*. Everywhere I go, I hear people talking to other people about their dreams. The time is coming. The end days are coming near. This *is* the book to open your dream life. Learn from it and grow!

A precious family I love and adore lost their son a few weeks ago, Darren Davis (twenty-one years old). As one of my close pastor friends and I visited this family, they spoke about how they were really having some powerful dreams. I felt very sad in their home, but his death actually caused me to finish this book and begin my life's quest to visit as many churches and places I can to share with you this precious form of communication with God.

Think about how many millions or billions of dreams that you might say have been wasted because of lack of knowledge. To understand the basic formula that it is *God who brings us our dreams* opens up a new avenue to your life. Follow these instructions I have learned over *twenty* years; learn and grow from them.

In the last days, we shall dream dreams. Now that you've read and have taught this you can dream and just wake up and go, "Wow, bizarre," or you can learn how to communicate those dreams *back* up to God, asking Him to help you understand them.

And then when we're through with that, we can then go to God with request after request, asking Him to guide your life, help you with decisions, and lead you to His Scriptures to help you through this life here on Earth.

Think God.

Well here I have to share with you a problem I've found, and some of you will surely run into this snag too. Many won't, but some will. You see, you gotta think God to begin this deep communication with Him.

I've gotta admit, there are many days when I go to bed worried that the San Diego Chargers aren't gonna win this week's game. Or I wonder if those Padres can continue their streak and get back in the pennant race. But the thing is that thinking about who's on first won't get the job done of talking with God. You must *think God* to be playing on His field. That surely doesn't mean every moment. Heck, I still gotta root for those Chargers; I don't know why, but I do. But I also *must* get focused on God when it comes to my dream life.

Now don't get me wrong. Naturally I'm deep in this dream life, but I'm just being open and honest with you … there are days that I'm just trippin' over sports, my bills at home, or the vacation we're about to go on in a few weeks. *But* the only way God talks to me is if I give Him my *all*.

Don't forget, our Lord tells us numerous times in Exodus and Deuteronomy that He's a jealous God. I don't think He's going to bring me a nice dream if I'm going to bed worried about how many completions Philip Rivers is going to make this weekend!

You see, our God is an all-in kinda Guy. If He's sees your sincere and desperate for communication with Him, He will deliver.

Now here comes a bit of a twist, but I *must* touch on it: déjà vu. Many times in my life I have been in a situation where I surely could confide, "I've done this before." I might be at a restaurant ordering a cheeseburger when a friend says something funny and I say, "Hey, I dreamed that last night." And I believe I truly did.

I remember swerving once to avoid a serious accident. When the car *didn't* hit me and as my jaw dropped below my waistline, I said, "OMG, how did I *not* get hit?" *this* came to me: "Wow, I dreamt that last night." Has that ever happened to you? It has to me, plenty of times.

So what is it? Is there a part of us that can see bits of what's going to happen tomorrow? Listen, I'm sure not into any kind of crystal balls, nor do I believe in *any* sort of person or persons I can consult with to tell me about my future, but I do know this: that word *déjà vu* has been a part of my life *or* has hit my life on numerous occasions. So what's that mean? Let's look!

Let me say something to you in this way: God has never opened my eyes or given me a dream to show me the future, *ever*. My stocks go up and down just like yours. He hasn't given me a tip on the stock market, and neither has He thrown me an address of a magical property that will go up in price in the next year.

But I have found a property to purchase, and I've taken it to Him in prayer. I've prayed about it, I've read the Word seeking guidance, and then I've prayed before sleeping and waited for answers to prayers. But just like you, that comes down to just *knowing* that God directs my steps and that those steps are walked in by faith!

Again, one of my favorite examples of this is when a young man called into the talk show "Pastor's Perspective" (on KWAVE radio station) and Pastor Chuck Smith had a question directed to him.

The young man said, "Should I move to San Diego, or should I stay in Orange County? I want to do what God wants in my life, but how do I know?" Chuck's answer was awesome and perfect: "If God is consulted and if you are walking with God, loving God, and living your life for God, then wherever you go, you must *know* it was God who led your path." Man did tears run down my face when I heard that simple answer.

Trust that God is guiding your life. Trust that when you get down to pray and ask God to help you learn about dreaming, He will perform. Remember, this might take some of you longer than others, but He's not going to omit you from something He'll allow another to have. Granted, there will be degrees or levels of dreams. One of you might have a dream from God almost every night and the other maybe only once a week or so. But don't fret; just keep working at it.

But that déjà vu thing; I still have that happen now and again, but by being aware of my dreams as I wake every day, it's not as common as it was earlier. Maybe that was one of the catapults God placed in my life for me to be more aware of my dreams.

Be consistent in your prayers. If you've found a person in your life you are considering to be your mate, and then for God's sake, begin studying the Word. Find a church, worship together, and pray together, but don't allow just dreams to tell you whether that person is the one.

Remember, dreaming is the dessert in my relationship with God. It's not the meat, and it is not the staples I need to *have* that relationship with God … once again, it's the dessert!

As Shar and I flip businesses (buy and sell), I surely use my accounting skills and knowledge of life and business to help make my decision. I go to the Lord in prayer and look for His openings or closings of windows of opportunity, but *yes*, I do also pray about it and then wait for Him to give me a dream. *And He does.*

You, friend, are about to begin a new chapter in your Christian life and grow. Ask God for I'm going to say minor directions in your life, at least to start. It was like my first example of the neighbors who were fighting. I asked our Lord, "Should I interfere in their domestic quarrels or leave them alone?" His answer was clear to me. It was not only clear, but I had double confirmed by my grandson's dream just minutes after being in awe over my dream. Remember, Nick's dream brought tears to my eyes. God *really* wanted me to know I was on to something here.

I wouldn't start your prayer requests by asking the Lord if you should begin a ministry in India and quit your job of twenty-five years. I think that's probably not the right way to become an expert at this. Let's learn to dream and interpret your dreams. Have plenty of them, and then begin to ask God for certain directions or to give you a dream in regard to certain decisions in your life.

I'm excited for you. You should be too. God's blessings to you on this.

CHAPTER 8

In Closing

In an earlier chapter, we spoke of the gifts of the Spirit. If you remember, I mentioned that I have never had the honor of speaking in tongues. The Lord has heard my prayers for the healing of many an individual, but I have yet to lay my hands on anyone and see an instant healing or miracle. I have also not stood up in church and prophesied, nor am I a preacher or a pastor. You see, we all have different kinds of gifts, but the same Spirit gives us these gifts; they come from above (1 Cor. 12:1–11).

I am confident, though, that one of the gifts the Lord has blessed me with is teaching. I have been told countless times in my life that I make learning so easy. I love to read and grow, and I'm inspired, then, to pass on the things I learn to others. Part of the prerequisite of being a teacher, I'm sure, is just a deep passion to want to teach others to grow. For me, that comes from loving Jesus and then, I believe, the deep love I have for others.

Although love is a commandment (Matt. 22:36–40), it is also a gift that has been bestowed upon me, I believe, in great abundance. Of course, like any normal man, I love my wife, my two daughters, as well as my two grandchildren, Nicholas and Clarissa, and I guess everybody else we are *supposed* to love. But you know, God seems to have blessed me with a deeper love than some people I have met in my life. I seem to be blessed with a kind of love that just wells up inside of me and fills me with a burning desire to want to try to help every person I meet. But it's not me that's so loving; *it's Christ loving you through me.*

Just pause a minute and think about what shape this world would be in with more love abounding in it rather than the hate we seem to find everywhere today. With a true and deep love for people, even marriages would be stronger, and some of today's violence could literally disappear if hate weren't so prevalent in today's world.

Catholics and Protestants wouldn't be shooting each other over in Ireland. Now that's one I will never comprehend. The school or public shootings and murders that take place throughout our country are being committed by children who may not have been raised in homes with any knowledge of a loving and merciful God. If these children would have been taught God's love and the grace given to us by Jesus, this entire world would be a better place to live, especially here in the United States, but what a foolish nation we have become. The moment we took God out of our schools, our nation started a slow downhill spin. The United States is doomed to destruction—inner destruction, that is.

When I was a young boy in school, we prayed before class even got started. God was a part of each and every day at my Belden school in Canton, Ohio. The school principal had the ability to discipline us when we children became unruly. Now every teacher, every assistant, and every counselor must guard their every action because of fear of our country's lawsuits that are filed every day. Everything and everybody seems to settle their issues in the courtroom.

I am not writing this book to speak about end times. This may still be just the beginning of what is to come. All I want to make you aware of is that this country isn't nearly in the shape it was twenty or thirty years ago. Violence is stronger, winters are harder, summers are hotter, and people are meaner. Lawsuits fly like there's no tomorrow. I think God is going to make a real showing in the next few years—so hold on to your hats!

I was listening to some "on hold" music while waiting for a customer service representative of a large company last week. The song I was listening to was such a hard and dirty song, filled with words of killing, brutality, and utter grossness, that I had to wonder, *Who in their right minds would put this station on as their on hold selection of music?*

Before I close this (moaning) portion of my book, I want to briefly comment on the three Woodstock concerts in state of New York. This last one in 1999 was turmoil at its worst! Not only did the rampage occur like that of five years before at Woodstock II, but this time the crowd burned just about everything in sight. Most of the vendors not only lost their inventory, but their booths, cars, and trailers were all burned to the ground. Some businessmen lost their life savings in an event that went way out of control. Watching the news from California, I looked on as these semi-trailers, stages, and speakers burned because of an unruly generation of monsters this country is now raising up. The first Woodstock concert in 1964 was so much different than the ones in 1994 and 1999. It just goes to show that this country is headed toward more and more chaos. Other countries, especially European ones, are just waiting for us to collapse. And you know, I think we will! *If there's no change in the direction we are headed, we surely will fall.*

So can we get back on track? Can we, as a race or generation of people turn back to God? It was originally God's plan for us to be *so* close to Him, but He knows it is in our nature to sin continuously.

> **With man this is impossible, but with God; all things are possible with God.**
>
> (Mark 10:27)

So there is a point to all this: We must simply watch Satan do his thing to glorify the work soon (and even now) to be done by the Holy Spirit. But listen, the Holy Spirit has a showing Himself today too! He says to us that He will pour out His Spirit in the last days. So get with the program; here He comes. As the world gets stronger in its violence and in its ungodly ways, the Holy Spirit is allowing us Christians to get stronger too. Can you not see that? Each of you must work with each other to support the body of the church. And how do you do that? You must learn to grow and put forth a stronger effort into that growth. Don't just go to church on Sunday and call it a week; live God each and every day of your lives.

Read the apostle Paul's work as he explains to us that it is a race we are in. He never said to join up and then sit back. We are in a war, friends. We are fighting a struggle against powers and principalities that we cannot even see (Eph. 6). We must all pray, jointly and continually, for Christ's return and know that this will soon happen, but we must now get on our knees and *all* ask Him to please come, Lord Jesus.

We must make our best attempt to unite all of Christ's body, the church, in these latter times—not necessarily under one roof or one so-called religion but under one prayer, one accord, and one united understanding that this spiritual battle is getting stronger and stronger. The stakes are getting more and more intense. We must turn up the volume!

We must get stronger with the times!

It takes a lot of love and a whole lot of patience to tolerate society today, but as strong Christians, we can do it. At least if we pray together and stay together, we can keep the dike from falling in on us, as long as we understand that we are all parts of one body, and each one of us is an essential part to that body as well (Eph. 4, 1 Cor. 12).

Let us look at the history of the US wars and learn from them, because that is just what we're in right now—a war. Adolf Hitler was unable to be conquered by one or even two countries; it took the Allies to bring down the German Army. In the Japanese and Korean Wars, again, it took a united effort to bring down those forces. We, too, must now bond as one nation under God. I'm sorry to say, but when I speak of nation here, I do not mean the United States but the nation of Christians. The church, under God, must unite in prayer and get ready for the big battles that are to come.

Don't be wimps and hide in your homes waiting for the rapture to come take you away. It might not be here quick enough. Pick up your pitchfork, get on your knees, get yourself into a local church, and get ready for a war that will surpass all wars. This war will soon be fought in every town, on every street, and in every home. And it will not be a war simply of guns but a spiritual war. The battle lines are being drawn, and God is calling every Christian together, *now*, to unite. If you have not been to church in a while, then we'll call you a reservist, and you know what? It's now time for the reserves to be called up.

In my younger years, I often questioned God's love for us. You might call this a bit of a confession, but I wasn't born a teacher; God made me one. I had to work hard to get to where I am now. Before we close, here are a couple of good stories to close on.

Shar and I went to an outdoor Mexican café one day in 1982 in Escondido, California. We were talking over lunch, and I was angry at God. I was explaining to Shar how God says He cares for us *more* than the birds of the air, yet He feeds them daily.

> **Look at the birds of the air; they do not sow or reap or store away in barns, and yet your heavenly Father feeds them ...**
>
> (Matt. 6:26)

We were going through some really hard financial times, and I said to Shar, "Yeah, He takes care of the birds all right, and look at them; they never have any problems." No sooner did I finish those words than a small sparrow flew right *onto our table* and sat there; we looked at it with our mouths open. Then I looked closer and saw the bird only had one leg! Tears rolled down both our faces as we beheld the glory of God.

For that bird to have been eating on the ground near us, I would surely have understood, especially a timid sparrow. Even in Venice, Italy, where we have seen thousands of birds eating under everyone's feet, but those were brave pigeons. Sea gulls, too, are a bit courageous, but sparrows are the most timid of birds. For them to come close to the table is one thing, but to land on the table? Well, that's altogether God. And then for it to have a foot missing! What a chill! What an experience! What a God! That bird flew right onto our table and looked right up at me … and only had one leg! Freaky!

The true life experiences I have had with God would take more than this book to document. But it is not my experiences I want you to read. You see, I want you to live your own life and have your own good time with God, but what I hope to teach you here is how to look for Him. He's there. Do you see Him? Remember how I told you that feel I live my life, every day, just like Abraham, Moses, and Noah. God is alive and in my life just as He was in their lives. Every part of every day, I see and walk with God. Oh, I don't literally see Him, but acknowledging my walk with Him allows Him to indeed better communicate with me.

God is as much alive and next to you as He is next to me. Please don't ever forget the dream I told you about when God came out of the rip in the sky, above my head. "I'm right here," He said. "I'm *always* right here." I know He wasn't just talking to me but to you too.

I am so grateful to my mother for the ways in which she taught me when I was a young lad. It took many years of bumps and bruises, but God saw me through all of it. I learned early how to recognize Him in the day and in the night. I might not have jumped on Mom's lessons early in life, but the cool thing about learning is you can recall the things you've learned (almost) at any moment.

Here's the other story: When I moved to Escondido in 1978, my three-year-old daughter, Christina, looked through our backseat car window (in her car seat, of course) at this church as we passed it on the freeway. All of a sudden she yelled out, "Daddy, Daddy, there's our church." Mind you, we had never attended this church, and in fact we hadn't even settled into the community yet. We were renting a house forty miles away from Escondido when we passed this church she called "ours."

We had just moved a few months earlier from Canton, Ohio, and we were looking *all over* San Diego County for a nice home to buy, and not just in Escondido. Out of the dozens and dozens of churches we would pass *every day* of the week, Chrissy looked over at this *one* church and said, "Daddy, there's our church."

Three weeks later, after passing that particular church about three different times, her response always the same: "Daddy, Daddy, there's our church again." I would look over at her and say, "What a weird kid."

But then it happened; we finally found a home we liked and told the real estate agent to make an offer. We came to find out the home we were making an offer on belonged to the pastor of a church! We didn't know it at the time, even during the offer we made. But one day, Pastor John Swartz of Bethel Baptist Church of Escondido said to us during our negotiations, "I'll let you have the home at the price you offered under one condition: you come to my church and visit us for three months." I smiled and asked him, "What church is yours?"

He answered, "Bethel Baptist Church. It's down the street about a mile, right off the freeway." He pointed right toward the direction of *that* church Christina had been calling "ours" for like three weeks. When he pointed over to what church it was and I realized what had happened, I about fell over. I literally cried right then, right there in front of everybody.

Here is how I look at my life, friends, as well as how I look at God in all of our lives. Our lives are all like a movie. The movie studio takes a year or so to produce this movie. When we rent or buy the movie, we watch that movie, which took years to make, in like two hours. We can watch it all the way through, or we can pause it and watch a little now and a little later. We can even watch it over and over again, if we so desire. If we get to know the movie well, we are even familiar with what scene is coming next and know the ending.

So here's the parable: We are the movie, and it is God watching the tape. He can play your tape, or He can play mine. He can pause yours and play mine. He can play yours and pause mine. And please understand this; God's time is not our time. He lives in a no-time zone, so He can watch our lives anytime He wants to.

> **A thousand years to the Lord is like one day and one day is like a thousand years.**

> (Ps. 90:4)

I have lived my entire life believing that my prayers and my life are just like that tape. Have you ever prayed and thought, *How can God hear my prayers when so many people are praying?* Time is standing still for God; He hears, waits for, and wants *all* of your prayers … *and* all of my prayers.

When I wake up each day, I walk, talk, and think about God, as if I am *the only* person in the world He's watching right then. I have virtually grasped the reality that God's time is not the same as my time. He can watch each of our lives one at a time or in groups (like at church), as families (at the dinner table), or He can watch everyone at once. He can watch reruns of us, pause us, fast forward us, and most scary, He can turn us off and allow the lights to go off in our lives!

So if you can grasp this, and I believe that is the way it is, then think about this: *God is waiting every moment for you to talk with Him.* He is standing there waiting and caring for you and only you! He wants to see you read His Word, pray (talk) to Him, as well as allow Him to speak to you in your dreams. He wants you to understand those dreams, too, because without that, what's the purpose of it all? Then He wants to wake you at night and speak to you *and you alone* just to have a relationship that He once desired out of even Adam or Eve.

Instead of grunting and saying, "He hasn't time for my prayers," think about it this way: He's waiting every moment, every day, *just* for *your* prayers. God is right next to you, all the time, every single moment of every single day. He is waiting for you to let Him become a bigger part of your life … all of the time. You might say He has your life in His DVD player and He doesn't want to watch any other movie (life) right now other than yours. So now it's up to you to produce your own movie. Will it be a B movie, or will you deliver to Him an A movie?

God watches each of us, one at a time, as well as all together, at one time. Your entire life (movie) can last a blink of an eye, and in fact your entire life can pass in that split second because His time is not your time. *Or* He can really sit back and enjoy every moment of your fellowship with Him and bless your life more than you will ever imagine. Why? Because maybe now you've grown to realize that you alone can live a life with God. It is just you and Him—nobody else, just you and the Lord … so live it to the *max*! Don't allow time to have your life *fly* by in a split second. Take your time, and allow God to enjoy eternity with you even today.

You see, friends, God speaks to me through my little baby girl, through the flight of a bird, on a bumper sticker of a car, and in my deepest sleep. He wakes me at night to talk to me, and He waits for me with love and patience. Do you get that? He's waiting for *me*. God gets excited when I get up and I say good morning to Him. And He listens as I talk to Him throughout the day. He loves me more than *anything* in His creation because I know He's there, and He loves that I recognize Him … He's my closest friend.

Isn't it easier to love people and have a relationship with them when they acknowledge you? Now, *hey*, wouldn't you like that from Him too? *Stop now* and think really hard on this. Isn't that what you really want out of this life—a true and great relationship with God? There is a God who cares so much about you that He's there for you and *you alone. Well, that's the way it is!* Wake up, God is talking to you too!

Hey, I'm not His star pupil, believe me. Like Paul said in Romans, I'm the worst of sinners. But God even waited on me during those periods of my silence. He waited for me as I sat naked with a crack pipe in my mouth and a bottle of booze next to me. He's waited for me as I drifted in and out of a relationship with Him.

He's not only waited for me during the worst periods of my life, but He's also been sitting right there in that slit in the air, trying to tell me, "Manuel, I'm right here … all the time." God is now waiting for you to find Him more deeply now too. Think of this: What a waste of a movie for Him to watch an entire life go by with no sound. The movie's running, He's watching it, but it's simply a waste. You've not spoken to Him, so there's no sound to *your* movie. *Boring!*

Writing this book was a challenge in my heart. It took a lot of prayer and a deep search for the will of God. Dare a man tread on God's ways? Dare any man change God's Word or make his own interpretation of them? Going into this with that on my mind took *faith*. Any man can play it safe by simply living life day by day and *not* trying to be so bold as to author a book, but taking the words of Martin Luther, "Unless I am convinced by Sacred Scripture or by evident reason, I cannot recant. For my conscience is held captive by the Word of God and to act against conscience is neither right or safe. Here I stand, I can do no other, God help me."

My first love is for Jesus. He is the Way, the Truth, and the Life. *Nobody gets to God unless they go through Jesus* (John 14:6). God has made it so simple, yet there are so many issues people deal with, and then they read the Bible. But the book of Romans has the formula, folks, and therein you will find the key to opening the door to salvation, as well as the rest of the Bible. Read Romans; it *is* the key that opens what we call the Roman Road. Then read it again a second time, and then move on to book of John. Romans 10:9 is your key Scripture. I'm not going to write it here; I want *you* to look it up!

There are statistics out there that say if you *stay in and attend a church with your spouse,* read the Bible together, *and* pray together, the odds of divorce are like five hundred to one or some astronomical figure like that. Can you imagine a world, or even our own United States, where marriage is bonded by success odds of five hundred to one?

Pastor Greg Laurie spoke once on how a kiss in the morning from your spouse raises a man's earning potential, as well as raises the percentage in keeping his marriage together, and it even helps a man stay at his job *and* tolerate his bosses more. And he went on to further explain how funny it is that *one* morning kiss can do so much for a man. Just a kiss! Just love!

I wake each and every morning hours before my wife, Shar. Before I rise out of bed, I put my hand on her and say these words aloud, "God, thank You for my wife. I love her so very much." I do this every single morning without fail. Sometimes I'll just say that, but most mornings I then go into a short prayer. You see, I do love her so much, as well as my two daughters and Nicholas as well. I love my granddaughter Clarissa too, but she went to be with the Lord.

I love my father more than he will ever know. My sisters and nieces mean so much to me too. I love them deeply. I love my in-laws more than they will ever be able to conceive. And I have so many friends, who I love so deeply too … And I love life itself. Thank You, God, for what You have blessed me with: love!

Folks, it's time for the Holy Spirit to come down on us in His full force. I believe the Lord has conveyed this to me in my dreams. Now I'm telling you, it's your time to accept what He has to give you. This is the main purpose of my book: to make you aware. I want you to experience this relationship with God at night, in your dreams. The heat is being turned up. We now need the reserves to come in out of the rain and grab onto the weapon of unity. Satan is fighting a strong battle, and we, too, must join in the battle against him. The Lord has put upon my heart that in these last days, He will speak to us through dreams as well as His Word.

The first and second centuries were really strong times in the Holy Spirit. So also are the twentieth and twenty-first centuries; watch and see. Let's call these the book-end centuries of this generation—that is called today. So get on your armor and prepare for Satan to fight even harder. No more excuses; no more words like, "Christians are hypocrites" and "I can get my religion at home," or any of those other stand-offish lines that are just excuses to not get up, get dressed, and go into training. God is calling you up into service. Will you respond or stay seated on your couch? If your country called you to defend it, would you sit on your couch at home and call everyone a hypocrite, or would you grab your gun, hit the streets, and defend these United States of America? To say you're a Christian and not be an active part of Jesus would be like joining the Marines and not showing up for duty.

If you really want this relationship with God and you want Him to come to you in your dreams, it is very necessary that you read His Word every day, as well as pray to Him throughout the day, and *be part of the family of God.*

Above all that, you *must* also share in a responsibility to vote in our public elections and take a stand on things that affect the way a Christian would want this country to be run. We have our own rights, and we need all of you to be an effective part of a speaking community, so don't be a couch potato! When a man makes a commitment to something, any kind of commitment, he must go through with it. Saying you are a Christian are only words until you make yourself part of the family of God.

Marriage, work, social clubs, adoptions, volunteer work, and everything else that would constitute a commitment are all necessary obligations, and you must get up *off your seat* and prove yourself worthy of the obligation in which you have entered. Commitments are one of the last great words we have today. There used to be a day where a man's word was everything. Whether it was a business deal, selling a car, or even trading goods, these were all done on a man's word. Today we use attorneys to complicate every deal, and I am so sad over this. When a man makes his own commitment, his own word, to join or to be a part of something, it is still his word, without contract.

There is *nothing* that is joined without later producing a type of service or commitment to the thing you have joined. It is the way.

In the book of Acts, before we were called Christians, we were called, the way (Acts 9:2, 19:23). It is my prayer that the way makes a comeback and we unite in His way, the only way, once again. We must make an attempt to help hold the body together. We must try as hard as we can to not allow the body of believers to break up any more than it is. If I had my way, every of Baptist, Pentecostal,

Lutheran, Presbyterian, nondenominational believer, or whoever else to all become committed to what the disciples started two thousand years ago.

The way was how we got started—and I believe it is the way that needs a comeback. I can't see our churches changing their names, can you? No. But what I do see are groups of organizations like the one I have belonged to since 1978, called CBMC (Christian Business Men's Committee). This group of men, in over fifty countries worldwide and all over our United States, has been committed to following the Lord and service to Him in a unique way. At CBMC, we don't ask what church you belong to, nor do we attempt to recruit you into our way of worship. However, each of these men is committed to follow and serve the risen Savior. I have been a proud member of this group for many years. They may not realize it, but they are the way.

God be with you in Christ, and remember—wake up! God really is talking to you!

Pleasant dreams!

> **Amen, Come Lord Jesus. The grace of the Lord Jesus be with God's people. Amen.**

> (Rev. 22:20b–21)